THE BEST OF
LITTLE SPOUSE ON THE PRAIRIE

Copyright © 1993 by Bedford House

All rights reserved. No part of this book may be reproduced or transmitted in any form or by any means, electronic or mechanical, including photocopying, recording or by any information storage and retrieval system, without written permission from the publisher.

Library of Congress Catalog Card Number 93-70817
ISBN 0-9636248-0-6

Bedford House
P.O. Box 210726
Bedford, Texas 76095

Printed in the United States of America

DEDICATION

I dedicate this book to my mother, Denzal Jean (Hanna) Reagan (1927-1983), who gave me the best start in life any child could have and more than enough love to last a lifetime.

ACKNOWLEDGEMENT

I want to thank Mel, my renewable energy source for these little anecdotes, for his love and support, and my dear Eric, for his patience during my "growing up" years.

Also, I am grateful to my marvelous, functional family—my very special father, Tommy, the only person in the world that thinks I'm perfect; and my baby brothers, Curry and Lyle, who know I'm not, but love me anyway; to Brenda, Debbie and Bev, who help keep the men in my life happy; and to Granny Hanna, a truly virtuous and inspiring woman whose life has been devoted to her family and the farm.

To all my other friends and relatives, including the Robinson clan, I say you are absolutely the best! I appreciate all the encouragement.

A special thanks to W. Leon Smith and J.W. Smith for giving me my first "real" writing job at THE CLIFTON RECORD and to my friends at Texas Farm Bureau for making "Little Spouse on the Prairie" a featured column. Thanks to my talented friend, collaborator (and soon to be neighbor) Vern Herschberger.

I would be remiss if I did not acknowledge the wonderful folks these stories are about, and the wonderful folks who read them. Many thanks. God bless you all.

FOREWORD

The tales you are about to read are true. Any similarities to any person, living or dead, are not purely coincidental. These are real people—some of them, REAL characters. And the predicaments have been downplayed because I simply don't have enough space to tell everything.

Bear in mind that my observations do not necessarily reflect the views of the management—depending on who is really in charge around here. But they do shed a little light on why there is never a dull moment at our house. However, I must say high adventure is not all it's cracked up to be, not unless you get a thrill out of sliding backwards down a slick slope in Ol' Green or find trying to outrun an angry bull while dodging cow patties and anthills a titillating experience! Still, life out here in the country is hard to beat—rattlesnakes and all.

One thing is for sure. My perspective is not the same as my husband Mel's. He'd tell the tales about him quite differently and some he wouldn't tell at all.

Poor Mel. He often complains, "My life is an open book." Well, here's the proof...

TABLE OF CONTENTS

NEW ATTITUDE 1
LOST AND FOUND 2
GOOD COP/BAD COP 4
IDEAS AND INVENTIONS 7
SHORT ORDER COOK 9
LANA SCISSORHANDS 11
HORSE LAUGHS 13
DUMB MOVES 15
OL' GREEN 17
CORNBREAD TRAP 19
COUNTRY CULTURE 23
KING OF THE PROCRASTINATORS 25
AGRICABULARY 28
MEL'S GONE HAYWIRE 30
FASHION ETIQUETTE 32
SANTA STORIES 35
FARMESE, IF YOU PLEASE 37
STACKING Zs 39
TELLTALE SIGNS 41
SONGWRITER ASPIRATIONS 43
MEL'S NO WIMP 46
HOG KILLIN' TIME 48

MISPLACED MODIFIERS	50
CANNIBAL	53
CITY SLICKERS	55
THOSE SLY DOGS	57
SOMETHING BORROWED	59
ARE WE HAVING FUN YET?	61
MR. POPEJOY'S BATMOBILE	65
MEL'S SHOPPING TIPS	69
A BUNCH O' BULL	71
FATHER KNOWS BEST	73
PUT LITTLE SPOUSE IN THE WHITE HOUSE	75
KING KONG 'COON	77
TAWKIN' TEXUN	79
MEL'S WALLHANGER	81
MEL'S NEW YEAR'S RESOLUTION	83
MEL'S MAMMOTH GARDEN	87
WHY IS IT?	88
MAKING BELIEVE AND MAKING MEMORIES	91

The Best of Little Spouse on the Prairie

"NEW ATTITUDE"

It's nice to be appreciated, but sometimes I wonder, does "Honey, I'd rather have you help me pour cement as anyone I know" qualify as a genuine compliment with other women? Or do gifts of new tires and tool sets give other wives the warm fuzzies?

Actually, I have become more suspicious of my husband since I overheard him telling a neighbor that he was going to buy me a new ax, "what with the cedars getting out of hand and all." Not that I don't know how to use one, you understand.

In 1977, we bought 100 acres on the Brazos River in northern Bosque County (Texas). It hadn't been farmed since the forties and was overrun with wild plum thickets, cedars and mesquites.

At the time, our son Eric was about 10 years old. Melvin's well-laid plan called for Eric to drive Ol' Green—our illustrious pickup—through the pasture, straddling the small cedars. I was to trail behind with an ax, whack the bushes and throw them in the pickup bed—all in one motion.

Meanwhile, Melvin assumed the more difficult task of sitting in the cab of his tractor, which was hooked to a root plow.

When we completed clearing the land, I had callouses on my hands while Melvin's were mostly...well, you figure it out.

Anyhow, I began to notice that Eric and I were the ones that had to stand in the way of openings Melvin didn't want the cattle to go through, while he drove them our way from the seat of Ol' Green—horn blaring! After a while, it was just me blocking the way of some charging cow. (Eric caught on

1

quicker than I did and, once he was old enough, always managed to be gone at cow-separating time.)

That's why I balked on my husband, recently, when he tried to butter me up to help him look for a cow that was hiding out in this wilderness-of-a-creek-bed in our front pasture. But to hear him tell it, I paid dearly for my new attitude.

"She made me so mad," he told a friend, "I locked her up in the house that night and slept in Ol' Green!"

"LOST AND FOUND"

Some folks stash money, but around my house, it's screw drivers and tack hammers. I stash the tools out of my husband's and son's reach so I can find them when I need them. They, on the other hand, manage to find and loot my secret stash and then hide the tools where NO one can find them!

When I was growing up, my family lived in a two-story house. If you were downstairs, what you were looking for was always upstairs and vice versa. And while my mother spent many long hours and shed a lot of tears trying to keep things organized, the Reagan clan always managed to foul them up again—and in record time!

The Best of Little Spouse on the Prairie

I swear, we spent all our time hunting for one thing or another. We had dozens of flashlights, can openers and other identical gadgets because it became easier to buy a new one than to look for the one that was lost.

This made me all the more determined to nip this foolishness in the bud when it started in my household. I stocked each bathroom with tweezers and nail clippers, and I made sure we had three different pairs of scissors for cutting hair, fabric and paper. And, to eliminate the need for jockeying wrenches and screwdrivers and such back and forth from Melvin's tool box to the house, I bought a separate set—including the absolutely essential Phillips screwdriver—for household use.

Next, I drilled Melvin and Eric, "If you'll put it back where it belongs, it'll be there when you need it!" Every time one of them asked me where the measuring tape or the WD-40 or the binoculars were, I reminded them of this fact. But, alas I too was fighting a losing battle.

Instead of the two-story house scenario, the situation with my boys became a matter of "when at the barn, whatever you need is at the house" when it wasn't the other way around. Eric would come sliding in sideways in Ol' Green and run inside, breathlessly announcing, "Dad sent me back to get the crowbar...have you seen it?"

Upon their return from the barn, the promise to retrieve the never-again-to-be-seen thermos left under who-knows-which shade tree—on the very next trip—was invariably made. And because I didn't secure them with a log chain, my tools—by ones and by twos—began to disappear, as did the tweezers, nail clippers and my best paring knife.

But revenge can be sweet. As a matter of fact, I sat back with a silent smirk while Melvin raked Eric over the coals for dismantling his tackle box, recently. (I still don't understand what all the fuss was about...I only dropped it twice between the stock pond and the house.)

Last Sunday morning, I decided to treat my little family to a breakfast of pancakes to smooth things over. While the hotcakes sizzled in my electric skillet, I ransacked the kitchen in search of a flipper. (Wouldn't you know it—my guys have been helping out by loading and unloading the dishwasher, among other things, ever since I resumed my career. And while the help is appreciated, they've totally wrecked my system of what goes where!)

Finally, I had to unplug the skillet and use a fork to lift out the first batch of pancakes, but better torn up than burned to a crisp, I always say.

Despite the fact that I'm still looking for the turner, the "pancake disaster cloud" had a silver lining after all...during my search, I happened to find three screw drivers, my sewing scissors and a "Rattle Trap" in the back of one of the drawers!

"GOOD COP/BAD COP"

Believe it or not, valuable lessons can be learned from watching television. Take the "good cop/bad cop" routine. We've all seen it at least a hundred times. The "bad cop" appears to be mean and merciless. The "good cop," by contrast, then sets out to convince the accused it is far better to cooperate with him than to fall into the hands of his ruthless partner. The poor sucker caves in and spills his guts every time.

Well, I told my husband if it works on TV, it should work in real life, so we decided to give it a shot.

It started with those annoying telemarketers selling aluminum siding. Melvin would let them tie him up on the phone for thirty minutes to an hour at a time. I never understood why he didn't tell them we lived in a rock house right off, but he didn't have the heart. So, I suggested we try the "good cop/bad cop" angle.

Now, he gets loose quick by telling them, "I really wish I had time to listen, but my wife is extremely jealous. She pitches a fit when she catches me talking on the phone...Lord help, I think I hear her comin' now!" and he slams down the receiver.

The same works in reverse. When those that are good (and regular) at trying to hoodwink me into taking on a project they don't want to do, I suddenly become the "good cop."

"I'd really love to help you out," I say, "but my husband won't let me. He's gettin' downright possessive, you know."

This tactic works best, however, when you're negotiating. You'd be surprised at the deals that can be made when you team up in this manner:

"Tell you what, I might can talk my wife into buyin' this truck if you'll throw in the air and put me on a trailer hitch...and maybe some other little extras...but I don't know...she seems to have her heart set on that little Dodge down the street."

Or when you're buying antiques...

The Best of Little Spouse on the Prairie

"My husband said if I can't buy it for less than $100, then I don't need it. I know that's considerably less than what you're asking for this chair, but..."

Same goes for property...

"It'd have to be a mighty good bargain to get my wife to move way out here in the boonies with the wildcats and rattlesnakes...It'll take some strong persuadin' on my part."

And it goes double for bankers and lawyers...some pretty good settlements and contracts can be accomplished if you can convince your attorney this act is for real. I remember overhearing our attorney telling the one representing the other side, "Melvin might agree to this, but I'm tellin' you right now...gettin' his wife to sign it is gonna be like pullin' teeth!"

Actually, we've been using this formula for years with our son without realizing it...

"Just wait 'til you're daddy gets home...he's gonna wear you out!" and "If it was up to me, Son, I'd say okay...but your mother says no" are just two examples.

Guess you've noticed by now that I'm the one who usually gets to be the "bad cop," huh? In our particular situation, it's more believable that way because of individual personalities. But generally, I think it's more effective when women play the "bad" role...I don't know if it's because men are more cowardly in confrontations with women than they are with other men or if it's because we really do know how to be "badder" cops than they do!

"IDEAS AND INVENTIONS"

My husband is the inventor in our family. He's come up with more "sump'neruthers" than you can shake a stick at—mostly born out of some situation arising out here in the "sticks."

Melvin said the statement about necessity being the mother of invention is true. He claims growing up too poor to pay attention and too far out in the country to run to town every time you turn around were compelling motivators for him. He also says if more people filled their idea bucket out here where both the mind and the view are clear, they'd have a better handle on it.

That all makes good sense, but I can't understand why he doesn't recognize the genius in my ideas for inventions. He can be a regular killjoy at times.

For instance, he failed to see the potential in my sponge car idea. I explained that with automobiles made of sponge, you wouldn't need seat belts or air bags or body shops because they'd just bounce off each other when they collided. Then the smart alec asked me if I had designed them to "weather" thunderstorms, pointing out that when soaking wet, the sponge car's top speed would be about 5 miles per hour.

I conceded that this was a minor engineering hitch, but that I was still working on it.

He also shot down my idea about compressed water, you know where you compress water in a capsule that, when opened, will fill a five-gallon bucket. I told him it ought to go over good. Hikers could just drop them in their backpacks or put them in their pockets and take them out as needed.

The Best of Little Spouse on the Prairie

Melvin called this idea insane. "There's no such thing as compressed water," he snorted.

"I know that...otherwise, why would I want to invent it?" I reasoned.

He glared at me. "What I mean is, it's impossible. It can't be done."

"That's what they said about going to the moon and running a four-minute mile...and coming up with a store-bought spaghetti sauce that tastes homemade," I argued.

I told Mel if water couldn't be compressed, then maybe we could dehydrate it into a powder so when you mix just a little water with it, it makes a whole bunch. At any rate, he wasn't too keen on that idea either.

I just can't figure him out. He doesn't seem to appreciate my marketing and enterprising schemes any more than my genius for inventing. He says my idea for starting a recycling business for old keys and bowling balls was almost as crazy as the one to sell politicians ad spots on milk cartons.

And he really hooted about my Persian Gulf pottery idea. In the fall of '91, when everything was at a standstill in the Saudi desert, it occurred to me that the soldiers could break the monotony by making pottery. I thought it could be a relaxing pastime, and the pottery could be sold back home to pay for the war. Anyhow, I told my husband all the soldiers needed to get going was a shipment of potter's wheels since they already had plenty of sand.

"That's crazy," he said. "And just how do you think they're going to haul enough water out there in the middle of the desert for them to make this pottery?"

I had to think for a minute. Then, a light bulb came on. "Man alive!" I squealed. "There's a ready-made market for my compressed water!"

"SHORT ORDER COOK"

Remember when families actually sat down and ate meals together...and they all ate the same thing?

I sort of remember those times.

Most of the time, my husband, son and I eat in individual shifts because of our schedules, and sometimes, in twos if we're lucky. But even then, I've noticed we seldom have the same foods on our plates.

Even in our pre-microwave days, fast food restaurants had already conditioned my family, to some degree, into wanting their own custom meals. It first started at breakfast.

"Dad said to cook his eggs over easy, and make mine scrambled..."; "I'll have bacon instead of sausage..."; "toast instead of biscuits, only toasted under the broiler, not in the toaster..."; "no oatmeal for me, I feel more like a Pop Tart."

Then I really became confused when my husband would say "I'll have a roast beef on whole wheat with mayo" and my son would chime in, "I'll have the same as Dad, only make it ham and cheese on white bread...dry."

Before you know it, I had become a short order cook! I suddenly found myself tailoring recipes, making some brownies with pecans, some without...some with frosting, some without...Jello with fruit, Jello without fruit...meatloaf with onions...meatloaf without. Talk about confusion trying to keep all the orders straight!

Nowadays, with the microwave, it's mayhem in our kitchen around meal time—which is never any time in particular, just whenever the mood strikes. It's two or three of us opening and slamming the pantry and refrigerator door, dishing up and doling out leftovers, banging drawers,

The Best of Little Spouse on the Prairie

reaching for this and that, cutting, chopping, wrapping, peeling, gouging potatoes with forks, clattering silverware, clanging ice cubes, elbowing, kicking shins and stomping toes in the contest to see who gets to use the microwave first!

Afterwards, the race is on to see who gets the best seat in front of the television and whichever one of us gets there first gets dibs on what everyone else has to watch. Of course, some rules do apply here. If anyone gets up for any reason, the others can switch channels—provided they win the toss up for the remote control. (It would probably be less intense if I just gave in and let Eric eat and watch television in his bedroom, but we must have some semblance of law and order and the truth is, I don't want Big Red stains on the carpet.)

Yes, meals have become a contact sport in our home, and I sometimes think the days of "centralized kitchen government" with predetermined, uniform meals at regular eating stations were better than our new freedom-of-choice voucher (or perhaps I should call it "coucher") system. At least I do until those few occasions when we do have an old-style family meal. Then, I'm usually seething because I've had to warm it over and over until I can round everyone up at once to eat it.

I also recall those days when my husband, who was five times as big as our son at the time, would pile the same amount of food on both their plates and insist that Eric eat every bite.

In retrospect, I'm not sure doing it the old way was all that much fun. But it did have its advantages. All I had to do was threaten Eric with liver and onions or Melvin with chicken and dumplings and I could get them to do anything I asked.

"LANA SCISSORHANDS"

My grandfather was a farmer who supplemented the family income by barbering on Saturdays when my mother was a young girl. She grew up watching him cut hair, so it was only natural that she take up the craft. And she was good at it. She cut my dad's hair and my brothers', along with assorted relatives'—even when burrs and flat tops were in style—during the '50s, '60s and '70s.

Well, it seems the mantle fell on me. It's not like it was a religious experience or anything, but something just seemed to come over me, and still does, when I put a pair of scissors in my hand.

My first realization of my haircutting skills was when I was nine years old. That's when I whittled my 12-year-old friend's waist-length ponytail down to a "pixie" like Audrey Hepburn's on the cover of <u>Modern Screen</u>. (Three days later, when her mother stopped crying and her father sobered up, they admitted the hairdo was a close facsimile.)

Although I experienced a temporary setback from adults who failed to recognize and foster my haircutting genius (they hid the scissors from me), this daring feat launched my haircutting career. However, from that point until I was in my late teens, I had to settle for trimming split ends, bangs and spit curls.

Although my artistic talents blossomed, somewhat, when I began cutting my husband's and son's hair, my creative urges have gone largely unfulfilled. Except for the one time I talked Melvin into a perm and a brief period when Eric let me layer his hair, it's been pretty much haircuts as usual.

The Best of Little Spouse on the Prairie

Because there's just absolutely no challenge to it, I'm not as eager to cut their hair as I once was. The fact that three of the ten or so barber shop haircuts my husband has had have been since 1988 is a good sign that I've got "barber burnout."

It's a little frightening. Once before, when I balked at giving Mel a haircut, my impatient husband decided to do it himself. Boy, was that a mistake! He simply pulled off his cap, backed up to a mirror and whacked off every little wisp of hair that flipped up.

"You've ruined it!" I exclaimed, counting no fewer than fifteen gaps.

He became defensive. "I don't care," he said. "I don't have to look at it!"

It took me two hours to straighten out his botched up mess. Afterwards, I told him, "The way you shingled the back, I'd say you should have been a roofer, not a barber!"

All in all, I've done pretty well and only made one or two messes myself. One of those times, when Eric was about eight years old, I cropped the sides of his hair almost to the scalp, like you see some guys wearing now, only it wasn't stylish back then. But all was not lost. I gave him a new Dallas Cowboys' ski cap as a peace offering. He wore it for three weeks running.

Another time, I cut my brother's hair too short. I'd been used to cutting straight hair, and I always cut hair wet. His hair had lots of body and drew up when it dried. He had sprouts everywhere. (I still say that haircut launched the spiked hairdo craze.)

One thing I've learned. Men, like women, expect miracles from the person fixing their hair. Once Melvin said, "See if you can make me look like Tom Selleck."

I sighed and replied. "Honey, this is a comb I have in my hand...not a wand!"

The Best of Little Spouse on the Prairie

"HORSE LAUGHS"

Anybody else would haul a blind cow to the canners. But Melvin would treat her like royalty. I know this is true because we once had a cow with cataracts. She couldn't fend for herself on the range, so he faithfully fed and watered her every day.

We're talking about a real softie here. My husband's hummingbirds have a dollar-a-day habit...When he paints the eaves of the house, he paints around the bird nests. I've even caught him baiting mouse traps without setting them. You get the picture...

More than once, his vulnerability for the helpless and pitiful has gotten him in a pickle...like those refugee horses he once brought home.

The story's a real tear jerker. It seems a man's wife had left him penniless, and he had custody of the horses by default. As luck would have it, he had lost the lease on his pasture and was forced to sell the animals.

Out of the goodness of his heart, Melvin gave the man a generous $500 for a bred mare and a filly. Afterwards, my husband spent another hundred dollars at the veterinary clinic, just so they'd survive the trip home—or so he claimed. (He had their hooves trimmed. I've never even had a professional manicure!)

Having pulled them out of starvation, we were blessed with an additional little hayburner in the early summer of that year. Eric named him Bold Ruler. (Original, eh?) I called him Bold Rooster when I wanted to annoy my son.

13

The Best of Little Spouse on the Prairie

Anyhow, my altruistic husband got further satisfaction by pulling a practical joke on the former owner of the horses. I must admit, it was pretty clever.

Mel had received a glossy print photograph of a horse in the mail. It was actually a snapshot of a syndicated stud horse, but the stance of the animal made it impossible to determine its gender. The horse looked remarkably like Blaze—our mare—except this horse was several hundred pounds heavier and beautifully groomed.

Melvin cut the snapshot to fit in his wallet. The next time he saw the fellow who'd sold him the horses, he whipped out the photo.

"Looka here at that ol mare you sold me. Man, she's really come out of it, hasn't she?" he gloated.

The other guy did a double-take. "Looks like I let that little lady go too cheap," he said, rubbing his chin in disbelief.

"Probably so," Mel grinned, "but that's the breaks!"

Seems to me that his successful deception was little compensation for taking on a life-long obligation, but it was a golden moment as far as Melvin was concerned.

I know I'm running a risk by revealing my husband's little weakness. Every horse trader in the country will probably be pounding on our door. But if one succeeds in pawning off some ailing creature on him, maybe Mel will take a lesson from the guy who paid $50,000 for a race horse which died the week after he bought him. When he later came face to face with the con artist who sold him the horse, the swindler, fearful that the man he'd flim-flammed was going to fight, began to make apologies.

"Don't apologize," the man told him. "I propped that old horse up, took his picture and went all over the countryside selling chances on him. I raffled him off and made myself plumb rich!"

"But I thought he died," the puzzled seller said. "I'll bet the fellow that won him got plenty mad."

"He was a little bit sore," the other guy explained. "I had to give him his dollar back!"

"DUMB MOVES"

Sometimes, I think people really make life harder than it ought to be. Like those people, for example, who settled International Falls, Minnesota.

One Metroplex (Dallas-Fort Worth) weatherman always used International Falls as a point of reference for its record-breaking, sub-zero temperatures. My son Eric—back in the days when it was 10 p.m. and I knew where my child was—never failed to comment, "I wonder who the dumb suckers were that founded International Falls?"

Eric did not appreciate the obvious benefits there must have been in picking that deep freeze for a home. I'm sure there must have been some, although I can't imagine what they were either. I, too, have to wonder why pioneers chose a region with such inherent hardships.

Ever wonder why people decided to build cities on fault lines, in flood zones, on the edges of seas and the sides of volcanoes?

The Best of Little Spouse on the Prairie

It seems to me these victims would find life to be much simpler if they weren't always in the process of cleaning up and rebuilding or just plain worrying about when the next earthquake or tidal wave is going to hit.

Peace and safety, however, are not the only considerations in choosing a geographic location for putting down roots. Making sure you build your house upwind from the dairy barn isn't a bad idea either.

One problem is that you usually don't know what's important to consider until you've already messed up...like some of you who probably built your homes right out in a clearing instead of the oak grove. Now, you don't have any shade around your house for picnics.

But then, there's our friends who built their home in an oak grove. They have a metal roof and they say the acorns dropping all night long are worse than Chinese water torture!

Bet some of you live on the wrong side of the creek. When the creek's up, you can't get to town. That's pretty annoying, and you probably wish you'd built on the opposite side. Except on Sundays. Then you have a good excuse to miss Sunday School.

Small things like this can make life harder than it would be otherwise. Recently, I pointed out that very thing to my husband.

"We're crazy to always live west of town. Every place we've ever owned has been west..." I said.

"So?" he grunted, burying his face deeper into the newspaper.

"It means I have to face the sun in the morning and when I drive home in the afternoon, the sun is right in my eyes. If we ever move again, our next home will be EAST of town!" I announced.

"Hmmp," he replied, without one ounce of empathy.

Although he denies it, I could swear I heard him mutter something like "haven't you ever heard of sunglasses?"

🌱

"OL' GREEN"

There are some things you don't dare criticize in our home and one of them is Ol' Green.

Ol' Green is my husband's pet name for his trusty old farm truck—now in semi-mothballs, but still useful for haying cows, hauling brush and other odd jobs around the place.

Melvin has the same kind of affection for Ol' Green that cowboys of the Old West had for their horses. You've heard of these eccentric people that want to be buried in their cars? Well, it wouldn't surprise me if my husband didn't have the same thing in mind...or he might go for something a little more pretentious, like bronzing Ol' Green and turning it into a monument in our front yard. (Since he insists on parking it there anyway, I might go for that idea. Bronze would have to be an improvement over that icky green.)

Mel doesn't take too kindly to my insults about his virtuous old pickup. As a matter of fact, he has been known to cringe, snarl—even pout—over some innocent little crack I've made about his "junkheap on wheels." He's altogether too sensitive.

The Best of Little Spouse on the Prairie

For instance, anytime I go along with him in Ol' Green, I have to squeeze inside of it and meld with all the stuff on the passenger side. It can be downright uncomfortable.

He's got a virtual hardware store on the dash. I'm telling you, there's one of everything imaginable and two of some! Usually, I have to hold my feet up because he's got a log chain or a come-a-long or some tractor part in the floorboard. There's empty coke bottles, enough caps and gloves for a chain gang and a wad of receipts that could keep IRS busy well into the next century!

To me this is nonsense and I just have to say so. (I can't help myself.)

"I swear, Melvin Robinson," I once told him. "You've got so much crud in the cab of this truck, you couldn't haul it all off in its bed!"

That ruffled his feathers a little, but the truth's the truth.

The thing that upsets him most, however, is if I say anything detrimental about Ol' Green's appearance. I defend this by asking you to tell me what good thing could be said about an old beat-up pickup with both headlights punched out, the grill bashed in, the tail-gate bent, both mirrors stripped off and more scratches on it that a head-to-toe mosquito bite?

To make my point, I offer this observation concerning our late border collie, Lad. (Melvin just fumes when I tell it, but I'm going to anyway.)

Back when Ol' Green was driven into town, to the sale barn, the feed store and such, Mel would always instruct Lad to "load up." The loyal dog would obediently hop into the back of the pickup and off they'd go, dust a flyin'.

On one particular trip, when I was riding "shotgun," Mel was upbraiding me for making such a big deal about being seen in Ol' Green. (With its inch-deep road film and other "rugged" features, sneaking into town as part of a freak show would have been simpler.)

Anyhow, we sat out front of the feed store while Melvin went through his "shame-on-you" routine in which he tried to make me feel bad for saying unkind and "untrue" things about his beloved pickup.

When he was done, I told him, "If you think I'm the only one that's embarrassed to be seen in this eyesore, just look."

My husband's countenance hit rock bottom when he realized what I was talking about. Of all the humiliating things "man's best friend" could have done, lo and behold, Laddie had jumped out of Ol' Green and into the back of the shiny new red pickup parked right beside us!

"CORNBREAD TRAP"

Kids are pretty clever. They often get away with the things they do to adults just because they're so cute.

Years ago, our friend's three-year-old twins woke him up from a nap. They tugged on their father 'til he followed them out in the backyard. Imagine his reaction when he discovered that the kids had taken a paint brush and green paint and painted his new white Oldsmobile all the way around, as high as they could reach! Still, he said he didn't have the

The Best of Little Spouse on the Prairie

heart to punish them because it was apparent they were as pleased as punch with their masterpiece.

The mother of these same adorable twins installed a door latch up high—on the outside of the bathroom door—to keep them from playing in the bathroom. It seemed like a pretty good idea until they dragged up a chair and locked her inside one day. The only window in the room was too small to crawl out of, so she stayed in there for hours before the children finally let her out. She said she pled with them and bribed them in every way imaginable, but they just giggled and whispered and refused to cooperate.

Of course, the little darlings were forgiven...they were just too cute to spank...and besides, they were too young and innocent to know what they were doing. (Sound a little bit like Tweety Bird and Puddy Cat?)

Not only do kids get away with things because they're cute, but sometimes their cuteness can cause you to be taken in by them. This is an unfair advantage. Some of the kids can be downright crafty.

For instance, when Melvin and I first married—in our pre-farm days—he and a friend had extra jobs after work to try to make a little money. A house mover had contracted my husband and his friend to help re-situate and level the houses on property in a nearby community.

It was their usual custom to skip dinner and go over straight from work just to take advantage of the daylight. One particular afternoon, Mel was under one of the houses working when he was almost overcome by the aroma of fried chicken and just-cooked cornbread coming from the house next door. He said it was all he could do to stay under the house, seeing as how his stomach was growling like crazy.

About that time, a little boy squatted down and shoved a wedge of hot cornbread right under my husband's nose.

"Want some?" the little boy asked.

The Best of Little Spouse on the Prairie

Melvin sure does like cornbread, and you really need to keep in mind that he was awfully hungry that day. He eyeballed the cornbread with hot butter dripping down both sides. He said it was the most larrupin' lookin' sight he'd seen all day.

"I'd better not...it wouldn't be right for me to eat your cornbread," he replied, fighting the urge to gobble the cornbread right out of the little boy's hand.

"Go ahead," the boy coaxed. "I can go get me some more. Go on...take a bite."

Finally, Melvin gave in to temptation and accepted the cornbread. He took one bite and the child burst out crying. He ran back into the house and Melvin heard him tell his mother, "MAMA, THAT MAN ATE MY CORNBREAD!"

Needless to say, my poor husband felt like a sheep-killin' dog. And when he heard the lady say to her sobbing son, "Now, now...that man was probably hungry or he wouldn't have taken it away from you...let Mommy get you some more," Mel decided he'd better wait until after dark to come out from under the house.

The Best of Little Spouse on the Prairie

"COUNTRY CULTURE"

Kids growing up in the country sometimes get the fool notion that they've missed out on some of the finer things of life...you know, they begin to think they've been culturally deprived.

I recall once that my little brother and I had been invited to have dinner with a family from Dallas that spent weekends on Lake Whitney near our home. Curry and I were four and six, respectively. We were so excited we could hardly wait.

Mother gave us spit baths, combed our hair and sent us on our way. We only had to walk about a quarter of a mile, but we left a little early. It wouldn't be polite to be late.

Just before noon, we knocked on the door. When it opened, our weekend neighbor did not look at all happy to see us. She explained to us, in an abrupt and condescending manner, that she had invited us to "dinner," not "lunch," and instructed us not to come back before 6 p.m.

The implication was that uppity city folks, who referred to the three meals as "breakfast, lunch and dinner," were correct, while we backward country bumpkins mistakenly observed "breakfast, dinner and supper," in that order.

("Well, I may have been born at night, but it wasn't last night!")

I was old enough to be embarrassed by the social blunder, although I was still confused as to what we had done wrong. My poor little brother, however, was really hurt by the rejection. I tried to console him by telling him that we could come back and eat later...that we had just come at the wrong time. But he cried all the way home, arguing, "It is TOO dinnertime!"

The Best of Little Spouse on the Prairie

If you wanted to split hairs concerning social graces, you could say we were just two "ignorant" little kids who acted according to what we'd been taught. The lady, on the other hand, was "enlightened" concerning proper mealtime etiquette, but she sure could have used a lesson or two about tact and courtesy from our country friends.

So who is more refined, country folks or city folks?

My totally biased opinion is that country folks have more culture by far and the following example proves it.

A friend of mine, who grew up in Milsap, Texas, and his wife, as college students, lived on a shoestring budget. Consequently, they lived on a steady diet of peanut butter sandwiches and red beans.

Upon graduation, Jean got a job and Terry was accepted into law school at Tulane University. To celebrate, the two cashed her first paycheck and decided to treat themselves to some of the finer foods they'd been missing out on while pinching pennies.

They'd been hearing their sophisticated metropolitan friends rave over a new food called "yogurt." It sounded so refined...so French...so cultured. Eating yogurt, they thought, must be a near-mystical experience that would be their rite of passage into "yuppiehood."

When the couple got home with this mystery food, they each got a spoon and sat down at the dinner table. Terry took one bite, then another. Brows knitted, he scanned the label on the yogurt carton.

Suddenly, he slammed the spoon down on the table and announced, "Shoot, Jean. This stuff ain't nothin' but clabber!"

I rest my case.

Exposure to city life can bring about a sobering reality for some of us. I've decided urbanites don't have anything we don't have, they just try to make us think they do by giving it a fancy name.

Never let city folks convince you that country folks don't have culture. We have plenty, and more than them, if you count sour cream, cottage cheese, buttermilk...

"KING OF THE PROCRASTINATORS"

Procrastination seems to be an inherent trait among husbands, at least that's what my friends and I have concluded. We get together over a cup of coffee, from time to time, and compare "honey do" lists. (A couple of the older ladies have undone tasks on their lists that pre-date World War II!)

The longer I live, the more I understand a plaque I once saw which showed a woman seated in an antique car with her husband winding up the manual crank to start the engine. The caption read, "The reason so many women are cranks is because men are such slow starters!"

Well, when it comes to "honey dos," my honey could pick up the pace a little bit. He's generally pretty thoughtful and does far more in the way of domestic chores than most of the men I know. But he still tends to put off certain dreaded assignments.

Mel always has a very good excuse for why he hasn't gotten around to obliging my most simple request. And he is convincingly repentant in renewing his vows to get around to it—*manana*.

I've explained to him that there are undeniable consequences to procrastination. "It does absolutely no good to wrap the pipes after they freeze and burst," I told him, prodding him to plan ahead.

I've also pointed out that an empty gas can when the lawnmower runs dry is as useless as a flat spare tire, a common "round tuit" out here where rocks and thorns are plentiful.

On the other hand, he has some pretty good arguments. When I remind him that the road to our house needs to be fixed, he replies, "It's only bad when it rains, and when it rains it's too wet to fix it."

Most winters, we don't have firewood. Each time I mention it, Mel says he's been meaning to get the blade on the chainsaw sharpened, but he just hasn't gotten around to it. And when I comment that a fire in the fireplace to warm up to would really be nice, he goes into a long dissertation on how inefficient fireplaces are and how they work against the central heat...blah, blah, blah.

I've tried to nudge him by preaching that putting off until tomorrow what he should do today creates more work for him down the road. I've been right, too. Case in point: I had been nagging him to move some bred cows to a leased pasture for months. By the time he got around to it, they'd calved and he had twice as many to haul!

Along the same lines, he didn't get in any hurry to get a new fence charger, although I warned him that the cows could come in and eat all the ground cover he was trying to get established in our flower beds.

Mel reasoned that the cattle wouldn't come near the fence anyway, having been conditioned with a jolt or two of electricity back when the fence was working. What he didn't take into account was that it had been so long since the fence had actually been hot, that a new generation of calves had not been conditioned. Sure enough, they broke into our front yard, tromped the flower beds and ate everything green in sight!

You can see that procrastination of this magnitude creates times that try women's souls. One of those times was when we lived on a little sandy land farm on the Brazos River.

We'd lived there going on two years and despite my pleas, I still didn't have any hot water hooked up to my washer. Our underwear and socks were beginning to look a dingy pink from the red sandy loam and my patience was wearing thin.

One day, along about March, I announced to my husband: "If you don't have the hot water hooked up to my washing machine by...er uh...September," I said, instead of "tomorrow," which is what I should have said but relented, "I'm leavin'!"

You can imagine that a harsh threat like that really tore up my husband. He expressed his sincere apologies and promised to do better and all that stuff. Then he asked, "Honey, if for some unforeseen reason I don't have it done by September, will you please give me an extension?"

Call me stupid, but I took one look at those big brown eyes and went out and bought a giant-size box of cold water detergent.

The Best of Little Spouse on the Prairie

"AGRICABULARY"

I've decided certain activities and problems are so unique to agriculture that there are simply no existing words to define them. So, I took the liberty to coin a few.

Either gender can identify with some of these while others apply exclusively to the menfolk. Perhaps you readers can add to my following "agricabulary."

blindhawglucksia—The enviable knack for being able to thread an 11 1/2-foot wide load through a 12-foot cattle guard.

bovinavolt—A cattle revolt led by one ornery and contentious cow your wife told you to haul six months ago.

bountadriponia—The mystical attraction surrounding pickups and farm equipment that lures you to change the oil and spark plugs while wearing your best Sunday clothes.

cashscramble—The regular activity of moving money from one checking account to the other to keep a step ahead of a rash of hot checks.

de ja pu—The illusion that you've already smelled a feedyard before you actually do.

dreadmill—The vicious cycle of having to eat tuna casserole twice a week because you lied to your wife about how good it was.

dropsimity—The likelihood that you'll step in cow poop just walking from the house to the mailbox.

droughtboggle—The ability of dry weather to persist beyond the limits of your worst imagination.

escapegoat—The goat that breaks out of the pen and manages to elude you when it's shearing time.

excessimajigs—The screws, bolts, washers—all left-over components—that you took off the tractor and couldn't figure

The Best of Little Spouse on the Prairie

out where to put back, but you didn't need anyway because it cranked up without them.

fumadooma—The overwhelming urge to see if you can make it to town on fumes when the gas gauge on your truck says "empty."

grovellycoo—The behavior and demeanor you exhibit while trying to sweet talk your wife into reducing the length of your punishment phase when she discovers you've spent the vacation money for a new shredder.

haybaleywick—The area of expertise belonging to the short-fused guy running a haybaler.

hissboomblahs—The blues associated with running over a stretch of road where—unbeknownst to you—the construction crew in the truck ahead spilled a box of roofing nails.

hoodspah—The rare ability to raise your head up while working on the pickup without bumping it under the hood.

howlitosis—Bad breath in cowdogs.

mumblyoops—The language that slips out when you accidently hit your thumb while banging on the tractor with a crow bar.

narcoflipsy—The consequences of falling to sleep at the wheel of your truck or tractor.

nukembull—The action you contemplate when your neighbor's excuse for a bull gets in with your heifers.

predicamentia—The probability that you will run out of propane in the middle of an icy spell because you keep forgetting to have the tank refilled.

reverse perturbia—The law that causes your trailer to always turn the opposite way from the way you want it to when you're trying to back up.

snickerception—Your awareness that one friend has offered a second friend a piece of pie who is unaware that it was sliced with the same knife the first guy uses to clean his fingernails and skin rabbits.

<u>stonewallesque</u>—An adjective that describes your slick finesse for making excuses when the same guy offers you a piece of the pie.

<u>straddlegy</u>—A dumb plan to straddle a cedar stump and cut across the pasture—when you're two hours late for supper—rather than take the long way around by the road.

<u>styrosnuffaphobia</u>—The fear of getting your styrofoam coffee cup mixed up with the one your neighbor spits his tobacco in during a hot domino game.

❧

"MEL'S GONE HAYWIRE!"

Two commodities that have revolutionized the world—at least my little corner of it— are baling wire and duct tape.

The fact that baling wire holds hay together is secondary to the many marvelous uses my husband has found for it. Melvin is so sold on it, I often say he's gone haywire!

For starters, baling wire is great for wiring gates shut, mending fences, tying up dragging tail pipes, or the float on the water trough—whichever the case may be.

Baling wire is dandy for holding a split hoe handle together. If you're clever, you could probably use it like a Slim

The Best of Little Spouse on the Prairie

Jim to trip the lock when you lock your keys up in the car. (I know for a fact it works good for fishing 'em out from behind the dryer.) In a tight, this miracle wire will also do for a car antenna, and doubled, you can roast marshmallows with it. (No sense in wrecking a perfectly good clothes hanger.)

Once, Mel used a piece of baling wire to fix our fireplace screen. To tell you the truth, you're liable to find it just about anywhere around our home.

Best of all, baling wire doesn't cost you anything. After all, you were going to scrap it (or leave it laying around out there in your pasture somewhere just waiting for some cow to get it wrapped around her foot; or to get it wound around the back axle of your pickup) after you pulled it off the bale anyhow.

Tied end to end, we'd probably have enough pieces of baling wire in the back of Ol' Green to reach to the moon and back. That sure is a lot of good wire that's going to waste in the back of that old truck.

As for the duct tape, it's not quite as cheap, but it, too, helps hold my family's little world together.

Duct tape has patched everything from lawn chairs to potty lids around our house. If I were manufacturing it though, I'd make it in designer colors. Silver is a little pretentious for my taste.

Duct tape is excellent for repairing holes in vinyl recliners, holding pictures in their frames, securing the newspapers, rags and plastic when you're wrapping outside water hydrants to keep them from freezing in winter, and light plumbing jobs. And, oh yes, duct tape can also be used for taping ducts.

A couple of winters back, Mel was bad about stomping out small embers that would spark out of the fireplace onto the hearth while wearing his houseshoes. Like the good wife that I am, I carried out my duty to inform him that he was going to burn holes in the soft soles of his shoes if he kept it up. Sure enough, I was right.

Imagine my surprise when, one morning, I happened to catch my husband with his feet propped up and noticed that he had new soles on his houseshoes. I scratched my head and squinted. Of all things, that ingenious man of mine had re-soled those silly shoes with strips of duct tape!

(Never mind that he could have bought a new pair for all the duct tape he used. Duct tape still came to the rescue.)

Yep, I'd say baling wire and duct tape are lifesavers when it comes to fixing things and making do. Add a can of WD-40 and you've got all the ingredients necessary to tackle just about any job.

"FASHION ETIQUETTE"

My son insists I am the only person alive who pays any attention to colors, fabric weights, and whether or not a particular article of clothing is appropriate for the season.

"Don't wear those white pants," I tell him. "Don't you know it's the dead of winter?"

"Who but you knows the difference?" Eric argues.

The Best of Little Spouse on the Prairie

"Obviously, fashion retailers...otherwise there wouldn't be summer clothes and winter clothes," I point out.

"It's just a gimmick to sell people more clothes," he counters. "Besides, I see white pants on guys all the time. And I saw several pairs of 'em in the store just the other day."

"Unless they were on the summer clearance rack, they were winter-weight pants. Yours are too light for this time of year," I insist. But he ignores me, pulls on his black turtleneck sweater and hiking boots and off he goes.

We have this conversation quite frequently around our house. And always, my son rolls his eyes and dismisses my fashion advice. But I give it anyway...it's kind of like a curse, this fashion etiquette (Eric calls it a hang-up) of mine.

I tell him I didn't make the rules, I just observe them. I didn't make the rule that says you should only wear white shoes between Easter and Labor Day. And the one that forbids the wearing of open-toed shoes in the winter. It wasn't me who said no hats on ladies after five...women over forty should not go sleeveless...straw handbags and canvas shoes only in summer...suede shoes only in winter...dress shoes and purses should match in color...dark cottons should be worn in the fall and pastels in the spring and summer.

I've done my best to indoctrinate my son (it's too late for my husband) concerning appropriate dress for men. I've preached felt hats are for winter, straw ones for summer...heavy caps for winter, mesh ones for summer (and none of them are to be worn inside, only outdoors). I've also kept Eric from making the worst fashion slip of all—wearing white sport socks with dark pants and dress shoes.

He thinks this is foolish, however, since he sees no reason to ever wear dress shoes. (We're talking about a guy who wore red Reeboks and a tuxedo to his senior prom!)

The Best of Little Spouse on the Prairie

And another thing...it sets my teeth on edge when Eric wears his favorite hot pink cap with his burnt orange pullover. "Why don't we wear our orange cap?" I prod.

"Let's don't and say we did," he retorts, donning sunglasses with apple red frames.

You can see that clashing color combinations and mismatched designs also fly in the face of my fashion dictates. But this child of mine seems to enjoy creating his own look by scrambling his shirts, pants and shorts around instead of wearing them with the ones purchased together as a set. (Drives me crazy!)

At least I know I've done my best. Regardless of how he dresses, Eric knows better...I've seen to that. But I still have this horrifying thought that he might make a fashion blunder that would defeat all my lectures...like one in particular that comes to mind.

Once at a wedding, and a rather extravagant one I might add, I noticed that the young groom—decked out in a spotless white tuxedo—was wearing athletic socks with white patent leather shoes. Eric says I was being entirely too picky to notice a little thing like that. But I ask you, how am I supposed to ignore those bright red stripes around the tops of the socks when they're glaring at me through those white pants?

Bet that young man's mother could have wrung his neck...and don't you know it made for some great wedding photos!

"SANTA STORIES"

I was in the fourth grade before I found out there was no Santa Claus. It was a devastating experience because I got into a tangle with my teacher over it.

I loved my teacher, you understand, but she assumed a great big kid like me knew there was no Santa when she shouldn't have. (Obviously, she'd forgotten how long it took me to learn to tell time.)

At any rate, I was the last in my class to know and I fought it tooth and nail and argued with her until I was blue in the face.

Not that I had never had any doubts. After all, you couldn't help but have a few if you'd seen as many six-foot-tall, hundred-and-twenty-five pound Santas with black horn-rimmed glasses standing on street corners in downtown Fort Worth as I had. But Mother assured me these were just Santa's helpers—not the real Santa Claus, who was extremely busy back at the North Pole. And I bought it.

That never worked with Eric. He would ask penetrating, provocative questions about Santa. Sounded more like a prosecutor than a little kid, with questions like "If Santa and his elves built this truck in his workshop, how come it says Tonka on it?" and statements like "If those reindeer had really landed on the roof, their hooves would have damaged the shingles." (The little skeptic.)

Anyhow, after the showdown with my teacher, I confronted my mother and grandmother. The two of them insisted that I had been right and that my teacher didn't know what she was talking about.

The Best of Little Spouse on the Prairie

To validate Santa's existence, Granny told me how Saint Nick had paid an unexpected visit to her house once when she was a little girl. She said he threatened to take her little sister away unless she and Aunt Kat vowed to be good and Uncle Carroll quit being so naughty. Well, I knew Granny wouldn't story to me, so I went straight back down to the schoolhouse and had it out with that teacher all over again. (Since the rest of those cowards in my class wouldn't speak up, I knew it was all up to me to defend Santa's good name.)

Mel got into a scrap on account of Santa once, too. When he was a little guy (many years ago), his older cousin stole his Santa Claus letter, climbed to the top of the windmill tower and stuffed it into the end of a pipe while Melvin stood below crying and yelling at him to bring it back.

After he was done gloating and showing off for all the other kids, the rascally cousin decided to come down. But every time he got close to the bottom of the tower, my husband, who was five years old at the time, swatted the teenager across the back of the legs with a piece of chain. Finally, Lynn went back to the top of the tower and retrieved the letter.

No doubt about it. Melvin said he was prepared to wallop him to death with that chain, if that's what it took, even though Lynn was twice his size. You see, tampering with a kid's letter to Santa is plenty serious business.

When Mel had the opportunity to play Santa in Clifton once, he had more fun than the law should allow. He flew into the municipal airport and rode into town from there on a fire truck—sirens blaring—to a local business where the children had gathered.

Afterwards, he was telling me of his various encounters with the kids, their reactions and expressions...and some of their unusual requests. I noticed a twinkle in his eye as he paused to admire his costume in the mirror, and I fully expected he was about to tell me one more tale of some cute little boy or girl climbing up on his knee and making some adorable comment.

Instead, Mel smoothed his beard and sighed. "You know, I've always wanted to ride on a fire truck," he said, "and today, I finally got my chance."

Some kids never grow up.

"FARMESE, IF YOU PLEASE"

Not long ago, I shared a few words in my "agricabulary" with you—"farmese" if you please.

I think just about everyone would agree that farming and ranching also has its own unique set of Murphy's laws. Here are just a few:

* When there's ice on the ground, the milk hand quits.

* The tractor part you don't need is always in stock while the one you want has to be ordered from the factory and it ends up coming two weeks into planting season.

* When your truck's on empty, the fellow selling the 99-cent-a-gallon fuel is out, but the one down the street has plenty for $1.27.

* The cows you don't plan to haul are the first ones in the work chute, while the ones you wanted in there scatter to the four winds.

The Best of Little Spouse on the Prairie

* Women: The rungs on the cattle guard are not far enough apart to keep the cows from crossing it, but just far enough apart that you fall through when you try to step across to open the gate.

* You have a fender bender in your pickup resulting in $499 worth of damage to it the day after you raised the $100 deductible to $500.

* For months, you've been praying for rain, and you finally get five inches the day you baled hay.

* You're driving along, singing the blues because the three new stock ponds you dug won't hold water, and you get stuck where the water stands in that low spot between the house and the barn.

* Wildcatters strike oil on your place and you discover in the fine print on your deed that you don't own any of the mineral rights. Afterwards, you make several attempts to drill a water well and keep on hitting oil.

* A storm comes through and blows down your new barn and leaves the old dilapidated one you've been intending to tear down unscathed.

* You can't get your pecan trees to grow, no matter what you do, but the mesquites and cedars do quite well (no matter what you do).

* On those rare occasions when you're lounging around in your drawers, the preacher comes.

"STACKING Zs"

Snoring is about as disgusting as anything I can think of. Everyone else must think so, too, because you can never find anyone who will admit that they snore.

When I gouge Melvin in the side and tell him to knock it off, he insists, "I couldn't have been snoring...I was awake," and immediately picks up where he left off without missing a lick.

Eric blames the noise coming from his room on some nocturnal creature outside his window. (Are there any wart hogs in Central Texas?)

It could be worse, I suppose. A friend says her husband's snoring sounds like a "poppin' Johnny," and my brother-in-law sounds as bad as a grain elevator when he catnaps on the couch. Melvin, on the other hand, sounds more like my coffee maker, with its rhythmic growling, sputtering and spewing. (However, there have been a few nights I thought they must have been blasting at the lime plant!)

My dad is the percolator type, too. His lips flap like he's blowing bubbles, and you hear more little puffs of air than snores. But sometimes the long lapses are a little scary. (When I was a little girl, I'd put my head on Daddy's chest and listen to make sure his heart was still beating between puffs.)

Melvin is one of ten children—nine boys and every one of them has a sister, his father always liked to say. Several summers back, the whole family—inlaws and outlaws, too—camped out on the Brazos River. When night fell, you never heard such a commotion in all your life! Those tents would swell and fall in unison as the nine men and some of their older sons, sprawled flat of their backs on cots and in

The Best of Little Spouse on the Prairie

hammocks and sleeping bags, stacked Zs the whole night through. (Must be genetic!)

Rumors at a nearby bait shop ranged from speculation that there'd been an all-night motocross that weekend to comments that a crew with chainsaws had been working around the clock to clear land for a new highline!

Recently, someone told me that you could buy a contraption for a snorer to strap on so that when he flipped over on his back, it would cause so much discomfort, he'd immediately turn on his side and quit snoring. I tried to find Mel one for Christmas, but the stores kept hanging up on me when I called to inquire. (Thought I was a crackpot.) And sales clerks gave me looks like they thought I must be crazy when I told them what I was looking for.

Since I was unsuccessful in my search for a snore deterrent, one of my projects this year is to create such a gadget from odds and ends around the house. I have a hard plastic brush that should do the trick, and I'm debating on whether or not to wire it on with baling wire or stick it on Mel's back with duct tape. (After a test run, I'll decide if I should patent it or not.)

As annoying as snoring can be, I can recall at least one instance in which I actually welcomed the sound. One summer night Mel thought it was cooler out on our deck than in the bedroom. He took a sheet and went out back to sleep, but rather than plopping down in one of the loungers, he took the cushion off, put it on top of the picnic table and stretched out there.

The next morning, I walked into the den just about daybreak. Since I hadn't had my first cup of coffee, I was still about half asleep, so you can imagine how startled I was when I looked out the patio door.

Lo and behold, Mel had pulled the sheet up over his head to keep the sun out of his eyes, leaving only his bare feet exposed. If there'd been an I.D. tag on his toe, I swear, he could have passed for a corpse laying on that table!

My heart skipped a beat and then pounded furiously as I moved closer. What a relief it was to suddenly hear that familiar, syncopated snore of his reverberating throughout the valley!

"TELLTALE SIGNS"

Melvin can deny it all he wants to, but when I wash his brand new dress jeans and three little holes appear in the crotch, I know he's been climbing over fences in them.

It's just one of those little telltale signs. My husband, who's been sternly warned about the consequences of doing farm work in his good clothes, has a closet full of telltale signs: twice-worn golf shirts with greasy spots on their fronts; long-sleeved western shirts marred by tiny little holes from welding sparks; dress pants with seats ripped out—not at the seam, but just to the right of it; snagged sweaters; T-shirts splattered with aluminum paint and others with rust on them; diesel-soaked dress shoes...

In each instance, Mel saw some little task that needed his immediate attention and since it was so piddly, there was no need to change out of his good clothes into his work clothes.

The Best of Little Spouse on the Prairie

Of course, not all his clothing catastrophes are his own doing...like when he wore his new insulated jacket to the sale barn and the guy behind him burned a hole in the back of it with a cigar.

Still, it seems as if it's inevitable that Melvin is going to ruin his new clothes the first chance he gets. The craziness of it all is that he thinks he can hide it from me.

For instance, when I ask him, "Is that a grass stain I see on those new pants?" he very innocently replies, "It's just the light in this room," and he quickly scurries away before I can examine them.

When I point out snags, he insists the fabric is supposed to be like that. He generally owns up to grease stains, but says he doesn't understand how he got them, seeing as how he was a good boy and didn't go anywhere near a piece of machinery.

Coveralls are absolutely useless in this instance since every little job that results in a rip or a stain was one my husband did not plan to do, but could not resist when it beckoned.

Once, upon returning from a short business trip, Mel decided he'd try to get on my good side by cooking supper. (He was still feeling a backlash for getting black smut off johnsongrass on the legs of his good white trousers and infesting his dress socks with beggars lice.) It wouldn't have been a bad idea except, as usual, he wasn't dressed for the occasion.

When I arrived home from work, I followed the aroma of fried chicken to the kitchen. As I rounded the corner into the dining room, I could see Mel, in true form, hovering over the range in his best three-piece suit, with a wide grin on his face.

As you might have guessed, two steps later—when he dropped freshly sliced, wet French fries into a skillet of hot grease—he was wearing a not-so-wide grinace. (That's an unmistakable expression somewhere between a grin and a grimace.)

"SONGWRITER ASPIRATIONS"

Melvin says instead of airing our dirty laundry before God and everybody, I should think about setting these stories to music like the writers of country western songs do.

He insists the songs would accomplish the same purpose, only people would have to pay to sing along. I could make a bundle, he says, and, at the same time, jumpstart the economy. (Mel says most C&W songs sound as if they were written by a frustrated gossip columnist anyhow.)

It occurred to me that he may just have struck upon an enterprising idea. Imagine...me...a songwriter.

Wouldn't you know it? I was flooded with inspiration last night, just about bedtime. One great song title after another flashed before me, like one continuous neon sign. They were coming so fast, I wanted to write them down before I forgot them, only I didn't want to turn the light on and wake Mel. So, I tiptoed to the bathroom and scribbled them down on a roll of toilet paper. It's a good thing too, because some have true potential. Here they are:

The Best of Little Spouse on the Prairie

"You're a Creep Feeder If I Ever Seen One"; "I'll Sell The Herd, Honey, If You'll Just State Your Beef"; "Knock Three Times On The Combine If You Want Me"; "Barn To Lose"; "The Last Word In Lonesome Is Moo"; "Thistle Be The Last Time"; "Your Bleatin' Heart"; "Fescue Me"; "I Been Steppin' In It More Than Steppin' Out"; "Ewe Light Up My Life"; "I Plowed From Daylight To Dark And Now I'm Playin' The Field"; "I'm A Broke Cowpoke From Roanoke"; "You're A Seedy Somebody"; "You Been Showin' Your Pesty Side"; "You're The Grains Behind This Bidness"; and my favorite, "She Threw A Fit When I Threw A Rod."

Maybe tonight, I'll get inspired to write some humdinger lyrics to go with them. Then, I'll need to line me up an investor to help me get going—you know, someone who recognizes and appreciates real talent. (If you know anyone like that, perhaps some farmer or rancher that's making money hand over fist and would like to back me in my songwriting career, maybe you could steer him or her in my direction.)

Just to show you how sincere I am, as an enticer, I'm going to give you a sample of my mindboggling songwriting abilities. The words to this song just came to me—like a bolt out of the blue! It's a real tear jerker—based on a sad story I overheard one guy telling another at the sale barn awhile back.

(Now, I'm counting on you folks to be honest and to show some self-restraint since I haven't got it copyrighted yet.) The title hasn't quite come to me, but I'm torn betwixt "Dippity Do Dah," and "Step-Over-Toe-Hold." The words go like this:

She's been dippin' in my bank account while I been dippin' snuff.

Makes no difference whether I talk sweet or whether I talk tough,

The Best of Little Spouse on the Prairie

She's been runnin' up my credit cards, and thanks my threat's a bluff,
And it's crystal clear that thangs won't change 'til I get off my duff.
(Ride) I'm perplexed...And sorely vexed.
From the state of things, I'd say I'm likely hexed.
She's been dippin' in my bank account while I've been dippin' snuff,
She's been spendin' all my hard earned cash and left me broke sure 'nough.
'Now the banker's breathin' down my neck and times are gettin' rough.
Tell me, how can I get shut of her and still keep all my stuff?

Now a friend of mine who knows the second cousin of the mechanic who works on the '63 Volkswagen that belongs to the woman who sews all those sequins on the cactus and tumbleweeds on Porter Wagoner's shirts critiqued this song for me. He says it shows real promise, that it's the stuff hit songs are made of...carefully chosen words that really "stir the heart and soul and challenge the mind," he said. All you need, he told me, are the right musicians.

(I'm not sure what he meant by it, but he mumbled something about a few hot licks on a fiddle and a whine or two from a steel guitar covering a multitude of sin.)

Call me square, but I like to involve my family in my success. And it just so happens that Melvin can play a guitar and a harmonica—at the same time. (He can do a lot of pickin' but not much grinnin'.)

It gives me goose bumps just thinking about all that fame and fortune that awaits me!

Now, all you potential backers, don't be too concerned if it takes me awhile to respond to your inquiries. I'll likely have

The Best of Little Spouse on the Prairie

to rent an extra post office box to catch the overflow mail. And if you try to call me today, I'll be out for a spell after lunch...I'm going to get me some of those European-wrapped fingernails, a cellular phone for my car, a tummy tuck and...oh yes, my bus ticket to Nashville!

"MEL'S NO WIMP"

By now, some of you may be thinking I'm married to a wimp, but you're dead wrong.

We're talking about a guy who liked to go up and down Ol' Grapey catching water snakes and filling up a tow sack with 'em when he was a kid. Afterwards, he'd pitch the sack into the swimming hole where the neighbor kids were having a good time—that is, until all those black snakes started crawling out! Once the kids were cleared out, Melvin would jump in and swim with the snakes!

My husband comes from a family that's tougher than toenails. When he was a little boy, he and his brothers' favorite pastime was taking paddle ball paddles and stirring up a swarm of bumble bees to bat back and forth with them. (Mel said just to make it a little more challenging, he'd wear a blindfold and handcuffs!)

Yep, the bottoms of that boy's feet were so tough, he could have walked on coals as a kid, but he mostly walked on

The Best of Little Spouse on the Prairie

grassburs and goatheads. Melvin said he never had on a pair of shoes until he started to school and when his mother insisted that he wear them, he thought she was trying to hobble him!

To this day, Mel hates overalls. Says when he was a kid, he had to wear them all the time. Once, when he was about five and his brother Roy was close to seven, their father had warned them not to be roping the calves in the corral by the house. The boys got to showing out for their cousins and completely ignored their dad's warning.

"I'm gonna rope that calf and whatever you do, don't turn aloose of the rope," Roy instructed his little brother.

First rattle out of the box, Roy roped the calf. He couldn't hold on, but Melvin managed to. The calf drug him 'round and 'round the pen. Every time it made a circle by the water trough, the bib of Mel's overalls filled up with another scoop of soupy mud and manure.

His mother had a fit when she saw him and started squalling at him to let go. You understand, Mel wasn't afraid of water snakes, or his dad's stern warnings, but he was overcome by cowardice when his mother carried on like that.

Now, the reason he hates overalls to this day is because she brought him a rub board and made him strip down to his underwear—in front of all his aunts, uncles and cousins—and wash those overalls right out there in plain sight under the windmill tower.

You can see my husband is by no means a wimp. He's risked life and limb on the farm. As a matter of fact, when Mel and I first married, he volunteered for a dangerous mission—to be a human head chute for my father. Mel suspended himself above the calves and then dropped down and straddled them, one by one, while Daddy vaccinated them. One of them, however, was a little boisterous and uncooperative. He happened to buck just about the time my father came down hard with the needle.

To make a long story short...Melvin will never have to worry about getting blackleg.

"HOG KILLIN' TIME"

Well, we didn't have any hog killin' weather this winter, that's for sure. But we did have some hog killin' stories around our house. Melvin's went like this...

"It was the early fifties...the year we made our first bale of cotton. We had proudly displayed our cotton samples by hanging them from the ceiling of the back room of our farm house.

"Grandma had come to live with us. Earlier that morning, she had stepped on a nail on her way to the outhouse. Mama planted Grandma in her rockin' chair where she sat and soaked her foot in kerosene for the better part of the day.

"Later that afternoon, Dad, Uncle Ewell, and some of the neighbors and older boys were hoisting a couple of fresh-killed hogs up on the bottom of the windmill tower to wash 'em and let 'em hang for awhile. We younger kids were playin' and marvelin' at the dead hogs while the womenfolk chatted and looked on—all except for Grandma, who was in the house soakin' her foot.

The Best of Little Spouse on the Prairie

"Meanwhile, My older sister Nona had gotten her jeans wet and went to the back room to find a dry pair. About that time, the light bulb burned out, so Nona struck a match and held it over her head to see. Instantly, a cotton sample went up in flames. Within seconds, the fire had spread to the others and my sister came runnin' out of the house shriekin', "FIRE! FIRE!"

Naturally, the men dropped the sows in the mud and broke out the water hoses, connecting them end to end to try to reach the burning house.

All at once, Mama realized that Grandma was inside. Then, she began screamin' and havin' a fit.

Several of the men ran inside, lifted Grandma—chair and all—and carried her outside to safety...I can still see her sittin' in that rocker, rockin' faster and faster as the excitement grew.

Anyhow, Dad manned the piecemeal water hose while the others attempted to save our meager belongings. Mama hollered and cried, mostly. Just when it appeared that the blazes were under control, the water ran out!

In a last-ditch effort to save the house, everyone grabbed axes, shovels, and corn scoops and began runnin' around in circles and attackin' that fire at a pace that put the Keystone Cops to shame.

When all was said and done, we lost the back room, along with all our clothes...that's where we kept what few we had...but we saved the house.

My sister felt awful about startin' the fire, but everyone was grateful that Grandma had been spared. Mama had a near nervous breakdown, but we did manage to salvage the pork.

"It wasn't funny back then, but when our family speaks of it now, we can't keep from laughin'."

The Best of Little Spouse on the Prairie

Hog killin' sparks memories for quite a few folks who've said they'd give their eyeteeth for a taste of fresh bacon, pork tenderloin, or a big ol' hunk of cracklin' cornbread. And it's awfully hard for them to relate to a generation of people who think "to render lard" is a religious term.

❦

"MISPLACED MODIFIERS"

Mel has made an irritating hobby of magnifying misplaced modifiers. When he's around, no one can get away with one of these perfectly harmless little grammatical errors.

Once, a friend's daughter made an attempt to carry on a conversation with him. "Guess what, Melvin. We saw a horse on the way to the farm," she said.

"Who got there first, you or the horse?" he asked.

Little Sara was puzzled by his response, but made another stab at it. "Guess what, Daddy killed nine rattlesnakes mowing the pasture!"

"Dear me, Sara. I hope he was smart enough to let 'em get finished mowin' before he killed 'em!" Melvin exclaimed.

Our son has also been the object of Melvin's warped sense of humor. A number of years ago, Eric arrived home from school one day and excitedly announced: "I saw forty deer on the school bus this morning!"

The Best of Little Spouse on the Prairie

Melvin was ready for him. "Now son, do you expect me to believe that? How in the world did they manage to squeeze forty deer on the school bus with all you kids?"

Next, Mel started in on me.

"Honey, I hit a fawn driving on the Norse road," I confessed.

I knew I'd slipped and said something wrong when I saw that gleam in his eye.

"Was he driving a car or a pickup?" he quipped.

"A motorcycle," I snapped. "Seriously, he smashed in the grill...up by the Necessarys' gate," I explained.

"Well, let's go up there and have a look at it," my witty spouse remarked.

"You don't understand," I growled. "This young deer jumped out in front of me on the way back from town!"

"And just how do you know he'd been to town?" Mel pressed me.

By this time, I was exasperated and really lost it. "Look, you nerd. I'm trying to tell you the front of the car is a mess. I hit a deer going 50 miles an hour!" I snarled.

Melvin grinned. "Man, that sucker was really movin', wasn't he?"

I have to admit, thoughts of homicide crossed my mind as I squinted at this smart alec. Finally, I suggested, "Would you please just come and look at the front of the car?"

He followed me out the door and inspected the shattered grill. After one look, Mel whistled. "I'd say from the shape of this grill, you must have hit the deer broadside."

Unable to resist, I dished it back. "WRONG! I hit him with the FRONT of the car!" I cackled.

Well, you know what they say about paybacks...

The Best of Little Spouse on the Prairie

"CANNIBAL"

People can call cows "dumb" all they want, but bovines are pretty clever when it comes to "resisting arrest." Few of them surrender easily when it comes to penning and separating them or moving them to a new location.

We once had a cow that was hooked on dry dog food. (Eric nicknamed her "Cannibal" since the dog food contained beef byproducts.) Anyhow, Cannibal would sneak up the bluff behind our house and force her way through a cedar thicket to get to our backyard and eat the dogs' food. (Before we figured it out, Melvin kept on worming the dogs. He thought worms were what was making them so skinny!) You could shoo her away or wave a broom at her, and she'd be back after the dog food before you could turn around.

Mel instructed our son to push the galvanized dog food pan up under our deck so the dogs could still reach it, but the cow couldn't. However, that didn't stop Cannibal.

The situation caused quite a commotion. Mel was sure Eric wasn't pushing it up under the deck far enough, but Eric claimed he was. Turns out he was, but the cow was kneeling down and dragging the pan out with her chin and then helping herself to the contents.

When it came time to rotate the cattle to another pasture, Cannibal hid out. The guys didn't discover it until we spotted her in the backyard later, crunching away at the dry dog food. But addiction to dog food worked against her. Melvin and Eric tricked the cow into getting into the trailer by putting the dog food pan inside. Then, they hauled her to the pasture where the other cows were wintering.

The Best of Little Spouse on the Prairie

One day, soon after the cattle returned the next summer, I heard the dogs barking and carrying on out back. I looked out the kitchen window, and there was Cannibal and her handsome bull calf, munching for all they were worth on dry dog food while she held the dogs at bay!

Another time, Eric had a show calf that kept getting out of his pen. Mel scolded Eric for leaving the pen open and warned him to be more careful. Again, Eric insisted he had made certain the gate was shut and couldn't understand who was letting the calf out. Well, the crafty calf was letting himself out. Mel caught him in the act. It seems the calf was taking his nose and lifting up on the bolt and then nudging it until the gate would swing open. So, they had to start wiring the gate.

Clever cattle are really hard to fool. My brothers found out with a handful of cattle that were wild as deer when it came time to vaccinate. When the cows saw Curry and Lyle together, they knew something was up, and my brothers couldn't get them to cooperate at all. The guys conceded that the cattle were pretty smart.

Finally, Curry instructed Lyle, "Get in the pickup and drive down the road a little piece and come back. Maybe they can't count."

Then, my brothers discovered if they set a trap where one of them hid behind a round bale or a tree while the other one stood inside the pen rattling a feed sack, the skiddish cattle could be lured inside. However, this was not always possible when there was no round bale or tree nearby.

But Curry came up with a solution. "You got duck blinds and deer blinds, why not cow blinds?"

Now is that a great idea or what?

My little brother's genius really amazes me sometimes. But it really shouldn't. After all, I taught him everything he knows.

The Best of Little Spouse on the Prairie

"CITY SLICKERS"

Through the years, I have been amused by the misconceptions and misnomers our city friends have had toward the rural life and experience.

One city gal admitted that she had always believed the blades of windmills caught water out of the air. Another one said she had been relieved to discover that when her fiancee spoke of "tanks" back on the farm, they were not military tanks but ponds.

Women are not the only ones guilty of these misconceptions. A neighbor said when her husband asked an urban friend who was down for a visit to go with him to check his heifers—which he said were "springing"—the guy fully expected to see cows hopping about in the pasture!

I've learned that some people believe peanuts grow on trees, just like walnuts and pecans. (The same has been said of cantaloupes and pineapples!) Others think sheep just naturally shed their wool every year.

If you believe the TV series "Green Acres" was an exaggeration, you should meet some of the people we've known who decided to leave the big city and find fulfillment on the farm.

One city slicker-turned-farmer couldn't understand why his week-old Holstein calves he bought at an auction were losing weight and wobbly legged. When my husband quizzed him, he discovered that the guy had bought the calves every kind of feed imaginable and couldn't get them to eat it. The novice farmer was quite impressed with my husband's astounding suggestion that perhaps he should try some powdered milk in a bottle!

The Best of Little Spouse on the Prairie

Later, the same guy showed Melvin a heifer he planned to take to the locker plant to be slaughtered the next day. Of course, my husband nearly dropped his teeth because it was obvious the heifer was about to have a calf.

"I don't believe I'd do that just yet," Mel told him, trying his best to downplay the guy's ignorance. "I could be wrong, you understand, but I'd be willing to bet she's going to have a calf any day now. As a matter of fact, I wouldn't doubt if she didn't have one by tomorrow morning."

The man was shocked. "Do you really think so?" he asked.

Sure enough, he called my husband the next morning to announce that the heifer had delivered a bull calf sometime during the night.

Eric has also had his experience with city slickers. Once, he and his dad caught some sandbass in the Brazos and shared them with one of these citified neighbors. She insisted that Eric come join them for lunch. The little guy came running in the house, all out of breath and eyes big as saucers, a short time later.

"How was the fish?" I asked him.

"I didn't eat any," he replied.

I thought that was strange since he liked fish so well, so I asked him, "Why not?"

"I couldn't eat that thing with it looking back at me!" he shivered.

As it turned out, the neighbor had cooked the sandbass like trout, head and all. What I wouldn't have given to have been a little fly on the wall when she set that platter down in front of him!

"THOSE SLY DOGS"

A young, raven-haired "home wrecker" has been making my life miserable! And to think my husband just picked the little temptress up alongside the road!

Things have not been the same since he brought Abby home. She gets all his attention and Eric is crazy about her, too. They say it's her effervescent personality—the little flirt!

Mel promised there'd be no more girls after Heather. She was the last one to come between us. And he's kept his word...until now. Of course, there was Laddie and Tippy and that destructive duo, Puddin' and Tane, who were equally bad about wallowing in my flower beds. Those sly dogs. Each one's mission in life seems to have been to make me crazy!

Mel broke the news to me gently...

"She looked so sad...so hungry...I asked folks up and down the road and no one claimed her. I just COULDN'T let her get run over. She's a beautiful little border collie...about three months old. Eric has just fallen in love with her."

"Now, I want to see you go home and look that little boy (Little, hmmmp. The Selective Service keeps raps on him.) in the eye and tell him he can't keep that dog," Mel poured it on.

Sure enough, when we got home, Eric was standing in the driveway romping and playing with Abby. Melvin whistled and the dog came running. Meanwhile, Eric followed me inside.

"Mom, it was so neat to come home and find Dad out in the yard playing with that puppy. You know how much he loves a dog and he misses Lad...surely you can't look him in the eye and tell him he can't keep Abby, can you?"

The Best of Little Spouse on the Prairie

Well, you know how it goes...those guys are suckers for puppies and I'm a sucker for those guys. But it's against my better judgment.

I recall how our last two Australian puppies excavated the yard. I came home one day to discover my caladiums shredded down to the bulbs. Naturally, Melvin and Eric challenged me when I accused the dogs of the dastardly deed.

"You don't KNOW that they did it. It could have been a possum or an armadillo...or cutworms..." the guys argued.

"What's a couple of goofy plants?" Eric added, taking the grocery sack from me to probe for a snack to eat on the way to baseball practice. "Just look at 'em. Have you ever seen anything so cute?"

My eyes wandered over the clutter surrounding this pesty pair. "Our backyard looks like a garbage dump!" I shrieked, taking inventory that included a mangled feed sack, an old boot, a piece of rope, a set of deer antlers and the sneakers I left on the back porch. "These dogs delight in mischief!"

"Yep, they're evil to the core," Eric retorted.

Puddin' was tugging at a crimson stalk while Tane was prancing around like a flamenco dancer with the convicting evidence clenched between his teeth.

Eric pecked on the window. The two furry, white creatures cocked their little heads and eagerly wagged their tails when they spotted us. Soon, they resumed their playful wrestling. Their antics were so cute, I felt my resentment wavering.

"You're right," I conceded. "What's a couple of goofy plants, anyway?"

Eric seemed pleased. "That's the spirit Mom. Better run."

He stuffed his wallet into his jeans and headed out the door. Moments later, the back door flew open. My son stood there fuming.

"What's wrong?" I gasped. Then, I saw the remains of a baseball glove in his left hand.

"It's those blasted mongrels," he snarled. "They don't have a lick of sense! I put this glove on top of the lawn table. How in the world could they have figured out a way to get at it?"

Trying hard not to smile, I offered my condolences. "It's those twisted minds...Who knows what those sly dogs will think of next?"

"SOMETHING BORROWED"

I am often amused at my husband's complaints that a friend, relative or neighbor has made off with his bow saw or sharpshooter...or crowbar. Of course, he never stops to take inventory of all the items he has that belong to someone else. The problem is, when these guys borrow tools and equipment from each other, they keep it for so long they actually believe it's theirs!

Like one of my dad's neighbors who once borrowed his small cattle trailer. It was in pretty bad shape, so the neighbor did a little light welding on it, replaced some of the lumber, added a couple of new tires...even slapped a little paint on it. By and by, Dad needed his trailer to haul a cow. The neighbor said, "Sure, go ahead." Of course, what Dad didn't realize is that because the neighbor had kept it so long and had fixed it up to where it hardly resembled its former self, the man believed he was loaning "his" trailer to my father!

It went back and forth like this for years (we called it a 'tweener), until the neighbor traded it in on a new one. Dad never said a word. He just continued to borrow the new one anytime he needed it.

Things don't always work out this well, however. A friend who moved to the city appointed my husband "guardian" over his chainsaw. He told Mel to use it as often and as long as he wished. Mel spent about $40 having it serviced and the blade sharpened. Before he even used it once, the man's son came and "borrowed" the chainsaw and Mel hasn't seen it since!

But you would be amazed at how many tools we've accumulated over the years that still linger. Mel is certain they all belong to him, but he is unable to recall just when or where he acquired them. You might say tools grow on trees around our place, mostly left there by friends or relatives building deer blinds or cutting firewood. Mel always intends to return them somehow, or expects they'll come back after them. But pretty soon, the tools are bouncing around in the back of Ol' Green with other odds and ends and Mel claims them as his own...like his decrepit old extension ladder.

Originally, my brothers' friend planned to get rid of the worn out ladder. Curry offered to haul it to the landfill for the friend. Soon, however, he and Lyle were using the rickety wooden ladder in their construction business. Mel stopped by one day to see how they were coming along on a metal barn and had a fit when he saw them going up and down the deathtrap ladder.

"You boys are gonna fall off that old ladder and break your necks," he warned. "The very idea...I'm gonna haul it off right now so you won't kill yourselves," he lectured, and threw the hazardous contraption into the back of Ol' Green.

That was eight years ago. Since then, Mel has climbed that deadly ladder to repair the roof umpteen times, to paint the house and to trim mistletoe out of 25- and 30-foot tall trees.

Bet if you ask him, he can't tell you when or where he got it, but you can bet your bottom dollar, he'll tell you that ladder's sure enough his.

"ARE WE HAVING FUN YET?"

Getting my husband to consent to what I call a "family vacation" is like pulling teeth. There is always something to be planted, picked, or plowed...calves to be weaned or vaccinated...or any number of things that need to be fixed.

When we finally do get away, rest and relaxation are the last thing on Mel's mind. To him, "R and R" stands for "rigorous and regimented." He has us up at the crack of dawn to hit the road and he has a glowing itinerary arranged.

I remember once he suggested we swing by Alamogorda, New Mexico on our way to Colorado. Eric kept whispering to me, "Only Dad would find it exciting to look at some old leftover bomb."

The Best of Little Spouse on the Prairie

Once we're buckled in, there's no stopping until we reach our destination. After three hours or so, I finally demand him to stop so I can go to the bathroom. That's when he peers at me over the rim of his sunglasses, asks "Why didn't you go before we left home?" and keeps on driving.

Fifteen minutes later, Eric jumps his father from behind while I wrestle him for the steering wheel.

Mel growls, "Oh, alright. But we won't make it before dark if we make these unnecessary stops!" Of all things, when we resume our tour, Mel hands me a hot dog and a 32-ounce coke!

If it looks like rain, my hubby starts in wondering who has hay on the ground back home or if I remembered to pay the feed bill. I remind him the purpose of the trip is to forget all that stuff and have a good time. Then he asks, "Are we having fun yet?"

About mid-afternoon, we've run out of snacks and Mel looks weary. That's when Eric or I offer to drive, but Mel squares his jaw and insists he can make it.

Eric whispers, "Ol' Super Bladder's afraid to let one of us drive. We might decide to check the plumbing somewhere."

Soon, Mel says something like, "I sure hope that number 84 heifer don't calve 'til we get back. I've been keepin' an eye on her."

We ignore him and silently pray he will heed nature's call soon.

Generally, we get behind a slow RV or a pokey driver and that just drives Mel crazy. So we have to listen to him griping about the roadhogs, why won't they move over, why it is they speed up every time you try to pass and how people like that should have more respect for other travelers and so on and so forth. He always concludes by saying he wishes he had one of those gadgets on his wheels like those chariot racers in the movie *Ben Hur*—you know, the ones that would reach out and ream all the spokes out of the other guy's wheel. Only Mel's would puncture roadhogs' tires and give 'em flats.

Naturally, we pass up all the decent-looking motels and finally wind up at a questionable one that's right next to a drag strip or a railroad track—so we have noises and tremors all night. It's clean, but the TV only gets three channels and the water pressure is zilch. That doesn't matter much though because the water is so hard you can't get the soap to lather anyway.

It always amazes me. Mel picks a place like this and then wonders why the beds are so uncomfortable. He told one cashier, "I rode that bed more ways than you can ride a hog side-saddle an' I just have to say that's the worst kinda torture I ever endured."

She still didn't give him a discount.

Of course, we start out the day with breakfast at some greasy spoon. And that's a big mistake, because Mel spots a tractor ad, an ad for bulls or $200-an-acre land for sale in the local newspaper. Suddenly, he decides to scrap the itinerary.

Somehow, separate "family vacations" are beginning to sound better all the time.

The Best of Little Spouse on the Prairie

"MR. POPEJOY'S BATMOBILE"

The first time I saw Walter Popejoy, he was dressed in nice jeans, a white western shirt and a bow tie. He looked perfectly harmless to me, and I'm generally a pretty good judge of character.

Anyhow, his neat appearance and genteel ways made it easy for him to talk my husband and me into going for a ride over his ranch in his old truck. I figured it couldn't be any worse than my many excursions with Mel in Ol' Green. Ha!

Mr. Popejoy had souped up his beloved "Batmobile" with a V-8 engine, special brakes and all kinds of concealed features. But just to look at it, you'd never suspect that old flat black, 1949 Ford pickup with a piece of plywood where the back windshield had once been, was anything more than an old clunker.

Once Mr. Popejoy had cast his spell and lured us into the truck, he cranked the engine and let it run for a moment. Mel and I were oblivious to the fact that we were about to be initiated into the select group, in and around Cranfills Gap, this prankster had previously duped into going for a ride in his hopped up "Batmobile."

Eric crawled into the back of the truck with three other unsuspecting souls and I was squashed between Mr. Popejoy and Mel in the cab.

"Away we go!" he suddenly announced, popping the clutch and smiling. I should have caught on when he added, "You're just gonna LOVE my Batmobile," a mischievous gleam in his eye.

The Best of Little Spouse on the Prairie

Just as we crested the first hill, "Evel Knievel" Popejoy took a sudden left turn and plunged to the bottom of a gully, pretending that he'd lost control.

I dug my nails into Melvin's forearm and braced myself for impending disaster, all the while thinking my poor baby in the back of the truck was going to be thrown out on impact!

About the time we should have hit rock bottom, Mr. Popejoy floorboarded it, and we sailed across the dry creek bed and began our ascent up the other side. By now, limbs were crashing, rocks were being upheaved and my eyes were big as saucers! Still, Mr. Popejoy acted as if nothing was out of the ordinary.

His well-rehearsed narrative began. "Now this is the Apache Trail," he said, pointing to the left, "And I call this one the Comanche Trail..." All at once, this sly little man shifted gears and went into a second nosedive. "AND THIS ONE'S THE MOHAWK TRAIL!" he yelled, appearing to have totally lost control of the "Batmobile," which was plummeting down the side of a rocky slope, contained in its path only by the stumps and trees on either side of a cleared out space along a fence row!

I muttered to Melvin, "Honey, I'll never complain about your driving again if we make it out alive!"

Meanwhile, Mr. Popejoy appeared to be fighting the steering wheel and jiggling the gear shift for all he was worth. He was working both feet and so was I, but it didn't seem to slow us down one bit!

Mel's face was the color of Ol' Green as we crashed down the hillside. (That was the only part of the PopeJOY ride I enjoyed—seeing my husband get a little dose of what he had put me through on more than one occasion.)

All at once, we soared through the air and dropped into a stock pond that had gone dry. Again, Mr. Popejoy stomped the accelerator and up the other side we went, with everyone squealing and hanging on for dear life.

Just when I thought the worst was behind us, Mr. Popejoy made a sharp right and off we went for a second trip around the bowl of the dry stock pond, over the edge and down again. Not once did this kidder let on like he was doing it on purpose!

Afterwards, I told my son I didn't know how he had kept from being thrown out.

"I had a 300-pound woman sitting on top of me most of the way," Eric exclaimed, "and BOY, was she mad! She said, 'Just wait 'til we get back to the house. I'm gonna CHOKE 'at li'l weasel!'"

Well, I don't suppose she carried out her threat because I got a phone call from Mr. Popejoy not long ago and he was doing just fine. Like that woman, I could have strangled him when we finally rolled to a stop and got out of the "Batmobile," but then Melvin pointed out, "It was every bit as good as 'The Runaway Mine Train' at Six Flags and it didn't cost us one dime!"

The Best of Little Spouse on the Prairie

"MEL'S SHOPPING TIPS"

I hate to shop in those super-duper supermarkets in the city—the ones that are big as football stadiums. You know how it is...you get all the way to one end of the store and realize you forgot to get prunes, and they're way down on the other end.

If you're looking for pickling lime, you could search for hours up and down those 100-foot aisles! Then, you ask a stocker and he gives you this blank look or he says he's going to go check in the back and that's the last you see of him.

After shopping in these whopper stores, hiking back and forth on the cement floors, herding a cart with those whoppy-jawed wheels...you need a chiropractic adjustment!

Afterwards, you stand in checkout lines as long as Great Depression soup lines, dodging the guy behind you who keeps running into your heels with his cart's front wheels. You watch your ice cream melt and listen to cranky babies bawl until you could just scream!

The worst isn't discovered until you get back home. That's when you realize the sacker set your gallon milk jug on top of your bread.

I prefer shopping in our small, hometown grocery store where I can visualize what's on every aisle and shelf. I can dart in there, find what I need and get out before dark. But my favorite way to shop is to give a list to Mel and let him take care of it. He really knows how to get the job done. Here are a few of his shopping tips.

Reading the labels is a must, he insists. He is a conspiracy theorist on this point. Mel says you MUST figure the price per ounce, that you can no longer assume the box marked

The Best of Little Spouse on the Prairie

"economy size" is a better buy than two smaller boxes of the same product which, together, contain more than the larger one. He is also suspicious of three-for-a-dollar tomato sauce and four-for-a-dollar biscuits, so he always calculates the unit price.

"Compare the sales price to the regular price," he warns. Sometimes, an item is cheaper when it's NOT on sale, he says.

Mel suggests you can get around the "two-per-customer" limit on sale items by having each family member pick up two and pay out individually. This, of course, is such an ingenious idea, I'm sure no one else has ever thought of it.

When there are only four fryers left at twenty-nine cents a pound, Mel recommends creating a diversion to get the woman about to claim them away from the counter long enough so you can sneak over and grab them.

Mel says the higher-priced items are usually placed at eye-level on the supermarket shelves. So, when shopping, he suggests you check the top and bottom shelves where the lower priced items are generally located. He says it pays to dig way back into the back and look for items with old prices marked on them, adding that they tend to get shoved back there. If you're lucky, you may find a real bargain. If not, he says the cans you've dinged up will be on sale in the bent-can cart the next time you come into the store.

One last tip. Mel says be sure to memorize your grocery list because if you're like him, you're apt to go off and leave it laying on the kitchen counter.

"A BUNCH O' BULL"

We once had a Charolais bull that was twenty-four hundred pounds of mean! Homer was his name and he had been on a rampage for days on end, running through fences, demolishing work pens and eluding everyone bent on his capture. He had even managed to get over on the school playground, which joined our leased pasture, and scatter the children! There was no doubt about it. Homer had to go!

Melvin did something he seldom does. He gave up! After days of dogging the troublesome bull, he finally decided to let some other fools give it a try. So he hired some cowboys to rope old Homer and put him in a trailer bound for the nearest sale barn. On the first day, Homer snapped two new ropes right off the bat! At dark-thirty, you could see the silhouettes of Homer and the cowboys, streaking across the horizon.

The next morning, the men resorted to a tranquilizer gun. Once the needle had found its target, the men with ropes moved quickly to force the belligerent bovine into the back of the trailer. But Homer planted all four hooves firmly in the ground and refused to budge!

Meanwhile, the men tied the ropes to the bumper of Ol' Green. Melvin got into the act and said, "When I pull forward, there's gonna be tension on these ropes like you never seen! Stand by...if he even looks like he's relaxin', rush him with those hot shots!"

Well, it worked. And that's how we happened to be hauling Homer to the Cleburne auction barn. Melvin had given Homer his walking papers.

The Best of Little Spouse on the Prairie

We deposited Homer with instructions for mailing us the check. But we soon learned our "Homer horrors" were not over. The frazzled man on the phone told Melvin, "YOU GOTTA COME DO SUMPTHIN!"

It seems Homer had outsmarted all the livestock commission employees; had run through a corral out back; and was now running loose in an adjacent pasture, terrorizing the cutter and canner cows!

When Mel arrived, he went straight out to the pasture and faced off with Homer. He may as well have been waving a red flag because when the beast recognized him, he pawed and snorted and headed right for my husband!

Mel made a run for the gate, planning to lure Homer inside his trap, but Homer was coming ninety-to-nothing. Just as my husband ran around the corner of the gate post, he slipped and fell.

Homer seemed to be smiling. Mel rolled over on his back and looked up just in time to see the charging bull hovering over him. Mel drew back his feet and kicked old Homer right between the eyes, burying both boot heels with all his might.

The bull was stunned. He staggered long enough for Mel to make a beeline for the barn. Moments later, Homer was hot on his trail. My decoy-husband led the bull to the scales and slammed the gate while everyone—including Mel—scrambled to safety in the rafters above.

In the end, Homer had to spend the night in the auction ring because that was the only enclosure strong enough and high enough to hold him!

Poor Homer probably wound up as hamburger meat. When I told Melvin it was very sad to think of Homer's fate, he merely replied, "BULL!"

"FATHER KNOWS BEST?"

"Now Son..." is a phrase I've heard many times over the years as my husband has shared his words of wisdom with Eric. More often than that, however, he has said, "Not that way, Son..."

You see, like many fathers, Mel just has to add his two cents worth, even when Eric is performing the smallest tasks. He believes HIS way is better...I always say Mel is like Ford—he has a better idea.

I must admit, some of Mel's little pointers make sense. Like "Now Son, always staple your barb wire inside the fence posts instead of outside so it won't pop off when the cows push against it." And, "Not that way, Son. Never plow 'round and 'round in circles without changing directions or you'll have so much dirt piled up along the fence rows, this field will look like a giant doodle bug hole."

But tell me, what possible difference can it make whether or not Eric opens a feed sack from right to left or from left to right?

Now that Eric is grown, he gets a little perturbed at his father's frequent suggestions. Not long ago, he said, "I can take airplanes apart and put them back together, but Dad seems to think I don't have sense enough to get in out of the rain. Would you believe last night he had to instruct me in the proper way to open a can of pork 'n beans?"

Because he is a lefty, everything Eric does looks backwards to my right-handed husband.

Eric confessed, "I know Dad means well, but he sure gets on my nerves sometimes. The other day, when I got out to

The Best of Little Spouse on the Prairie

lock the gate, he told me I put the lock in the wrong link of the chain. I backed it up one link and that satisfied him.

"Then we went to buy bait and gas. I pulled the Bronco up and he immediately told me to back it up a little. I did. Then he said up a little more, it was in the sun. I told him, 'Dad, it's not like I'm trying to dock the space shuttle!'"

"We drove down to the water and I picked up a rock to block the wheels. Wrong one. Should have gotten the one next to it. The fishing went the same way. First, I tied the hook on wrong. Since I couldn't bait it right, I decided to try a top water lure. But Dad said I was reeling it too fast. Then I tied on a "Little George" and he said I was reeling it too slow, that I was going to get hung.

"When I started to take the hook out of the fish's mouth—like I've done a jillion times before—Dad said, 'Not that way, Son,' and then he showed me HIS way, which looked exactly like MY way to me."

Then Eric grinned and said, "But I still caught more fish than he did doing everything wrong!"

I pointed out to Eric that Mel thinks he taught me everything I know, too, and that, as his wife and son, it is our responsibility to keep that delusion alive. After all, he is just trying to be helpful.

Eric sighed. "Yeah, I guess a lot of fathers are like that. I thought Dad had really gone too far when he said I didn't know how to hold a shovel right. Then a friend told me he and his father had been building a fence together and his dad jumped him out for stacking dirt on the wrong side of the posthole!"

"PUT LITTLE SPOUSE IN THE WHITE HOUSE"

After much deliberation with my family and friends, I am today announcing my candidacy for the presidency of the United States.

Mel told me he didn't think I had much hope of winning, but the way I see it—that hasn't stopped anyone else from running!

My campaign slogan will be: "Put Little Spouse in the White House November 3rd!"

I've asked my son, Eric, to be my vice-presidential running mate. He's an extra good speller. And I've already figured on appointing Melvin to the Supreme Court so I'll have at least one of the judges under my thumb. I'm still open for suggestions on Secretary of Agriculture.

Farm and ranch women will run my Office of Management and Budget. They've learned to squeak by on so little for so long, they should be able to run this country on next to nothing. And as president, I plan to cut a few corners myself. For starters, I'll get rid of Air Force I. Ol' Green will do just fine.

I have some other dandy ideas for controlling spending. Now tell me if this isn't a good one. Congress will have to run any over-budget items by your bank loan officers for approval. Now that ought to put the quietus on things!

Next, I'll cut the Stealth bomber—you know, the plane that's engineered to cross into enemy territory undetected by radar. Shoot, I can't see paying almost a billion dollars apiece for Stealths when we could equip one of those little drug

The Best of Little Spouse on the Prairie

runner planes with bombs for a whole lot less. They seem to come and go anytime they please without being caught.

As president, I'll combine the Environmental Protection Agency with the Department of Defense and kill two birds with one stone. I'll pack bombs full of the nation's dirty disposable diapers and drop them on Saddam Hussein.

I'll let farmers and ranchers write ethics laws for our state and federal officials. Wonder what they'll be able to do with their hands tied behind THEIR backs?

Little Spouse in the White House would fund research to make fuel from mesquite and cedar stumps; and to bioengineer some animals that will only eat weeds. Then we can turn them out and let them weed our gardens for us.

For my War on Drugs, I'll send a fleet of crop dusters to Columbia. (I'll make sure pilots are careful not to spray Juan Valdez's coffee beans.) And to assist states with prison costs and overcrowding, I'll convert all our old battleships into floating penitentiaries and have sharks for guards!

Finally, to reduce the deficit, I'm considering having people from all over the nation gather at a huge stadium and allowing the highest bidders to take shots at their favorite members of Congress in a series of events—including Water Dunks and Pie Throws. We'd make a bundle at the concession stands and if it catches on, the event could become a national sport to rival football and baseball.

I can only see one drawback. Sure as the world, some of those politicians will get to thinking they're worth as much as our athletes and start demanding the same kind of pay!

"KING KONG 'COON"

A couple of years ago, I was awakened one night by a creaking sound from above the bed. I shook Mel. "There's someone walking around on the roof," I whispered.

"You're dreaming. Go back to sleep," he replied.

I nudged him again. "No. Listen."

Mel was silent. Then he said, "must be a squirrel."

I sat up in the bed. "Sounds more like King Kong to me."

Mel didn't budge and soon, the commotion stopped.

A couple of nights later, I was sitting on the couch when I happened to see this gigantic raccoon drop down off the roof onto our deck rail. That explained what I'd been hearing. I didn't think much more about it until Eric came home a few days later and said, "There's a huge hole in the roof over Dad's office. Has he been cleaning his shotgun again?"

We soon discovered a pair of raccoons had selected our attic for their winter home and had torn off several sections of cedar shingles so they could get in and out. With rain in the forecast, the roof had to be patched, but for sure, we didn't want to shut the raccoons up inside our attic.

Eric was nominated to go up and run them out. Actually, he was the only one skinny enough to fit. He was equipped with one of those riot flashlights in case the 'coon crowd got unruly.

Meanwhile, Mel had borrowed my brother's live traps and had tacked them in strategic positions to catch the 'coons. Those metal cages all over our roof didn't do much for aesthetics, but my husband was bound and determined to catch those furry rascals.

The Best of Little Spouse on the Prairie

We solved that problem. Next, the critters started tearing the lids off our metal garbage cans and rummaging through the trash. It really disappointed me because I believed all that stuff about 'coons and their hygiene, you know, how they wash their hands before every meal and so on. My respect for them really fell a notch or two after that. And Mel got irritated when they ripped open a sack of deer feed and made a mess under the carport. So he drug out one of the trusty traps and rigged it with bacon.

Thirty minutes later, we heard the cage rattle.

"I'll take him down to the creek in the mornin' and turn him loose," Mel announced. But later, when I went out to take a look, the "varmint" was gone. Seems the crafty 'coon had chewed the springs and let himself out.

The next night, Mel was ready for him. Sure enough, about sundown we heard the animal scratching around in the cage. When Eric came home a short time later, his father asked, "Did you see that 'coon I caught?"

Eric ducked outside and returned shortly. "What'd you do with him? The trap's empty."

"Can't be. I wired it shut," Mel argued. But sure enough, the clever critter had managed to chew a small hole and squeeze through it.

The next day, our new neighbors reported that a 'coon had taken the screen off their RV, gone inside and stolen a loaf of bread. The last they saw of him, he was dragging the loaf down the hill toward the creek.

I suggested he might be planning on making himself some sandwiches with all the bacon he'd been ripping off Mel.

Afterwards, I asked my husband if I should put a couple of pounds of bacon on my shopping list, but he said he wasn't going to reset the trap. "He's too smart to fall for it again," Mel said.

"That's probably what the 'coon is saying about you," I grunted.

Raccoons are smart little boogers. I believe the "beatin'est" tale I ever heard was about a pet 'coon that loved sweet potatoes baked over coals. Supposedly, this 'coon would sit on the hearth of the fireplace, eagerly waiting for a yam.

On one occasion, the impatient 'coon and a calico cat were sitting side by side. The clever 'coon eyed a yam and eyed the cat. He could wait no longer. Suddenly, he jumped on the unsuspecting cat, grabbed its paw and plunged it into the coals to rake out a hot potato!

All I can say is the raccoons in our neck of the woods must be his descendants.

"TAWKIN' TEXUN"

Ah s'pose ya'll rillahz thur's sump'n uneek 'bout tha way Texuns tawk. If you don't b'lieve it, jes venchur outsahd tha Lone Star state apiece.

In Ioway, a wrench iz sump'n farmers use fer bangin' on tractor parts. Down here in Texus, a "wrench" iz sump'n beaudy operadurs put on li'l ol' ladies' hair to keep it from turnin' yellur.

In Areezona, tar is sump'n people spread on thur rooves and top with gravel. In theze here parts, we put that "tar" on

The Best of Little Spouse on the Prairie

tha gravel an' hope we make it to that hahway 'fore we git a flat!

In Noo York, the Yankees' pitcher hangs aroun' on the pitcher's mound. Down here, "pitchers" hang on walls.

Lahk me, Ah betchu've bin accuzed uv tawkin' funny by sum uv them East Coast emmygrunts, havun'tchu? They shore have a way uv makin' fohks feel seff-conchus. It eben makes you set up 'n take notice how ever'body else tawks.

Fer instunce, mah husban' Mel caws the fuzz the "PO-lice" an' caws that glass cuhver on a watch tha "chrischull" 'stead uv sayin' it proper. Ah do mah best to correck him an' 'learn him how to tawk raht, but it's a uphill baddull.

When Ah wuz a li'l girl, my granny wud say, "It's gonna commista rainin' dreckly," 'n shore 'nuff, it wud! (When Ah didn't heed her warnin', Ah'd end up wetter'n a drownded rat!) Then she'd say, "We're gonna have cump'ny," and when Ah asked who, she'd replah, "Evelyn n'em," an' shortly, Aint Evelyn an' her whole crew'd drahv up.

Ah usta have a friend that ate "aags" fer breakfus. (In the summertahm, she'd set in her porch swang memorahzin' scripchurs from her Bahble whahl eatin' "taters" and "maters" one raht after tha othur. Then, she'd warsh 'em down with "sodies.") She innerduced me onct to her uncle who wuz a plummer. He wuz constunly havin' to unstop "dreens." (But mah friend said her uncle towed her he'd "druther" be in "Gwadaleharr" with "SO-pheea Lowren" anytahm as to be a plum broke plummer fixin' broke potties.)

Ah got some West Texus friends who thank this cuhntry's too dependent on "oyal" from the "Ay-rabs." (One uv 'em ain't haff bad as a "sanger" and a "gee-tar" picker.)

Au cud go on ferever, but Ah thank you git that driff. Now, ya'll pleez excuze me. Ya see, Ah dun let my "arnin'" pahl up...Ah need to fluff "pillers"...an' Ah got this arful headache...but it shud be gone purdy soon caws Ah taken me a coupla "asperns."

❦

"MEL'S WALLHANGER"

It was about this time of year, back in the mid-1970s, when Mel, Eric and I decided to go fishing in a lake on our family hunting lease near Walnut Springs. The three of us were casting grape-colored artificial worms from a small aluminum boat and not having much luck. Soon, the wind caused the boat to drift out in the deeper water among several dead trees.

All at once, Mel's rod bent and looked as if it would break.

"Hold it," he ordered. "I'm hung."

That's when the drag of his reel began to whine.

"It's movin'!" he yelled, cranking that reel as fast as it would go.

My excited husband would stand up and reel for a while. Then he would pause and sit down to keep the line from snapping.

By this time, Eric, who was just a small fry, and I put our rods in the boat so we could watch the show.

The Best of Little Spouse on the Prairie

"This one's goin' on the wall," Melvin grunted, straining every muscle in his face. "Never had one fight this way before. It's got to be a big sucker!"

Whatever it was, it was pulling our boat all around the lake. Eric's eyes were big as saucers.

The tug-of-war seemed to go on for ages.

"I may need some relief," my exhausted husband finally groaned.

Forty-pound Eric excitedly volunteered to take over for his dad, but Mel seemed to get a second wind.

For the next twenty minutes or so, my ecstatic husband fantasized about the whopper on the end of his line. He went on and on about how he was going to be the envy of every guy in the Cleburne Bass Club. He was narrowing down the field of taxidermists to stuff the fish and had picked out a place above the fireplace to hang it. He concluded it would take Molly bolts to support it, but he had that taken care of.

Eric saw it first. "It's a turtle, Dad! A big one!"

When Mel laid eyes on that enormous algae-covered shell, he was deflated.

"Sonuvagun," he sighed, sinking back down into the boat.

The monstrous turtle hissed and splashed while Eric kept asking if we could eat him.

"You were right," I told Mel. "It's going to take railroad spikes to hold that on the wall."

He pretended to ignore me and instructed me to get an oar and start paddling for shore—turtle in tow.

"I can't let him go. He'll eat too many fish," my disappointed husband explained. "Let's pull him to the bank."

That trip to dry land was probably the longest of Melvin's glorious fishing career. Every breath, Eric had a question.

"Can we eat him, Daddy? What does a turtle taste like? Have you ever eaten a turtle, Dad? Can we make soup out of him? That turtle sure had you fooled, huh Dad?" he riveted.

"You thought he was a great big fish, huh Dad? What's that green stuff on his back? Wonder how much he weighs, Dad? Reckon he weighs a hundred pounds? How old would you say he is? I say he's 50 years old, how about you, Dad? Maybe I can take him to show and tell. Bet you can hardly wait to show him to the men at the bass club, huh Dad..."

"MEL'S NEW YEAR'S RESOLUTION"

Mel had his feelings hurt when I suggested he scrap the idea of making New Year's resolutions. We still haven't recovered from the one he made last year, which was to economize by doing things himself that he would ordinarily pay someone else to do.

I first learned of his money-saving vow when I caught him filling empty milk cartons and plastic jugs with water.

"It's ridiculous what they charge for bagged ice. I'm going to start making up my own so we'll have it when we go fishing or camping," he announced.

This continued for several months. Then one day, I was in the utility room when I heard this loud crash inside the freezer. When I opened the door, an avalanche of jugs came tumbling out. The brackets had broken and the freezer shelves had collapsed from all that weight!

The Best of Little Spouse on the Prairie

So much for cheap ice.

Then, I made the mistake of mentioning that the bottom oven of my range wasn't working. Mel's eyes sparkled and his chest bowed.

"I can fix it," he proclaimed.

The next thing you know, he had the stove out in the middle of the kitchen floor with the back off of it. My expert troubleshooter pinpointed the problem and ordered the part. Meanwhile, for the next three or four days, we had to maneuver around the stove.

When the part arrived, Mel installed it and reassembled the oven, all except for a few little pieces he insisted would never be missed. The oven still didn't work.

"It didn't cost much to see if I could fix it," he shrugged.

If you only count the cost of the part, his time and the inconvenience, I guess not. But now, I've got two little holes in the linoleum in front of the stove that weren't there before. (I haven't mentioned it to Mel because I'm not up to having him attempt a floor covering job.)

When Mel decided to level the washer and change out the belt on the clothes dryer, Eric began to get a little worried.

"Who does Dad think he is, the Maytag man?" he whispered.

The trash compactor was next. I don't know what Mel did to it, but ever since he overhauled it, the compactor grinds and whines and causes ground tremors when you push the start button. It can be quite embarrassing. (To keep guests from getting too alarmed, I just tell them the army must be shelling down at Fort Hood.)

I have to admit my husband has made some improvement as a handyman. Not long ago, he changed the bulbs in the recessed lights in our kitchen and the master bedroom and only broke one light cover. And he was actually able to get my blow dryer to run again after it quit on me. (I don't have the heart to tell him , but now it doesn't have enough power to blow out a candle.) But an old tractor he has been working on for over a year now still won't run. The problem is every time he fixes one thing on it, he breaks something else.

Recently, Mel spent the weekend reworking the commode in our bathroom. He changed out the float and all that stuff in the tank. It seems the water in the toilet wouldn't completely cut off, which he claims was the cause for our high water bills. But something still isn't right. Now, the commode gasps, and when it does, you hear a mysterious high-pitched whistle on the other end of the house. Something's going on in the pipes and it's scary to think what it might be!

But on the bright side, Mel's plumbing project has only cost us seven or eight dollars—so far. That's (1) if you don't count the patch of carpet that's going to have to be replaced because rusty sludge from the old innards oozed out on it; and (2) provided the finger he cut while groping around in the back of the potty doesn't get infected and rot off.

I told Mel, "No more lofty New Year's resolutions this year. Stick to something simple, something innocuous...like resolving to stop chewing toothpicks up into little splinters and dropping them behind the couch."

The Best of Little Spouse on the Prairie

86

"MEL'S MAMMOTH GARDEN"

Just once, I would like to have a regular-sized garden, but Melvin insists on plowing up a spot the size of a football field! He gets carried away planting everything from brussels sprouts to rhubarb, and then we all have to work like the dickens tending to this vegetable empire!

Melvin is like a little kid in a candy store when it comes to choosing seeds. It's an all day event. First, he polls every man, woman, and child that sets foot in the farm supply to get his or her opinion of which variety is best. Then, he ends up buying some of each, just to be on the safe side.

Afterwards, we mark off rows and heap up hills and count out seeds till doomsday.

When we were newlyweds, we had a really bad stand of nut grass coming up with our watermelons. Melvin sent me to the farm store to get something for it. Being a novice at that sort of thing, I relied on the clerk's expertise and returned a short time later with a sure-fire remedy.

Mel eyed the eight-ounce bottle in the sack.

"Man, this must be potent stuff. What's the ratio of dilution?" he asked.

"You don't dilute it," I explained. "The fellow at the store says to use the eye-dropper and apply a single drop to each little nut and that will permanently take care of the problem."

"You've got to be kidding!" he barked. "Do you realize how many bottles of this stuff we'd need and how many hours we could spend?"

"If we had a NORMAL size garden instead of a MAMMOTH one, we could probably do it," I reminded him.

The Best of Little Spouse on the Prairie

I recall that he made a big production out of the selection of tomato and pepper plants later on. And our first pickings of peas and beans called for a big celebration.

For weeks, every conversation at home and abroad revolved around which was best, raw-pack or water-bath methods, Charleston Grays or Mexican Reds. We canned and pickled until we had to cash in a C.D. to buy more jars! Everything else we ate in season (cantaloupe three times a day and at bedtime), gave away or crammed into our bulging freezer. We wore out four pairs of gloves, two hoes, the front burner on my range, and the canning manual I got from the county Extension office. If fall hadn't come to my rescue, I was planning to start a zucchini bread route!

I have warned Melvin there will be no more truck farms under the guise of a garden. I laid down the law. I put my foot down hard. We finally came to a compromise. This year, he's promised to cut out the rhubarb.

"WHY IS IT?"

Why is it that nobody wants a drink of water until you turn on the scalding water to rinse dishes? Ever notice that? You get the water real good and hot, and then you have to turn it over to the cold side to let them get a drink.

The Best of Little Spouse on the Prairie

This is one of life's many mysteries. And there's a whole passel more, like...

Why is it that the telephone always rings just as you sit down for dinner?

How come paper towels, business forms and garbage bags never tear on the perforations?

Why is it that when you get down to the last piece of cake or pie left on the platter, nobody will eat it?

How come it's easy enough for your cows to find a hole in the fence when they want out, but not when you're trying to get them back in?

Why is it ordinary people can go to jail for writing hot checks when the government gets away with it every day?

How come men have a natural aversion to putting a new roll of toilet tissue on the roller?

Why is it that foods you want to keep hot always get cold while the ones you're trying to keep cold get hot?

How come the highway patrolman let's the guy passing you go free and then pulls you over for going 65?

Why is it you never have your umbrella with you when you need it?

How come the cash register tape always runs out and has to be replaced or the checker closes the checkout stand when it's finally your turn?

Why is it when you can clean your house from top to bottom, nobody ever sees it but let it go just one time and company drops in?

Why is it the food you spill on yourself is never the same color as the clothes you have on?

You're expecting mail with a check in it and it gets returned because two digits of the address are switched. Why is it that never has stopped you from getting bills?

The Best of Little Spouse on the Prairie

Why is it that you can't set a digital alarm clock without passing by the correct time at least twice and loosing your cool before you finally get it right?

How come the kids — without failure — spill milk right after you wax the kitchen floor?

Why is it that people always eat more when they say they're not hungry?

How come your pen always decides to give up the ghost when you're trying to jot down a telephone or license plate number?

Why is it company always waits to drop by when your house is in a mess?

How come you doze off just about the time the news and weather comes on and then get wide awake when you go to bed?

Why is it that kids can open child-proof containers, but adults can't?

How come politicians promise you the moon before an election, but all you can afford afterwards is a moon pie?

The Best of Little Spouse on the Prairie

"MAKING BELIEVE AND MAKING MEMORIES"

Ever notice how small children are often more fascinated with the box a Christmas toy came in than the toy itself?

When that happens, it really makes you wonder whether or not all that fretting and knocking yourself out to find that special request was worth it.

I don't know a single person whose life has been ruined because Santa didn't bring a certain gift. Although Saint Nick was always generous to me, I am sure he could not always find or afford everything I may have wanted as a child. Yet, I don't recall ever being disappointed.

Looking back, my little brother and I seldom played with toys anyway, other than Lincoln Logs and Tinker-toys. Curry's dump-truck and road-grader were fairly entertaining, and on rare occasions, we would play with Mr. Potato Head. But most of the time, we were much too busy to play with inanimate objects.

On warm days, Curry and I would go exploring, collecting fossils and rocks we were certain bore mysterious markings left by Indians. We never ended one of these expeditions without picking our mother a bouquet of wildflowers—mostly weeds. She would pretend to be delighted and would immediately put the wilted flowers in a container of water.

I remember once when we decided to dig through to China. We had Momma's good silver in the back yard scraping away at the caliche. We didn't make much headway, even though we poured water on the spot to try to soften the limestone hill we'd selected for digging our tunnel. I think we gave up when the hole was just about five or six inches deep—just right for Daddy to step in and turn his ankle when he was mowing.

The day was not all lost, however. Afterwards, I taught my little brother to print the names of everyone in our family and many other essential words for a three-year-old boy to know. Fortunately for me, Daddy had just painted the new carport and shed stark white—the perfect background for the demonstration of my superior writing skills. And it must have been my lucky day because I found some charcoal which made excellent "chalk" for my "blackboard."

Before dark, Curry and I had worked our way around the building, scrawling letters and names as high as our little arms would reach. (We looked like coal miners by this time.) We were pleased as punch when we stood back to admire our graffiti. As I recall, however, Daddy was not particularly impressed.

I told Curry we'd better lay low for a few days, so the next day we played with the dog for a while. Afterwards, the two of us decided we'd play dead and see if we could trick the buzzards so we could get a close look at them. We had a bad sunburn to show for it, but we never could get those stupid birds' attention!

When it was too wet or cold to play outside, we loved to play inside a huge cardboard box, or sometimes, beneath a card table covered with an old blanket. The two of us would entertain ourselves inside our "tent" while Momma went about her housework. Here, our imaginations got healthy workouts. We didn't even come out to eat—Momma would fix us picnics—except for the time Curry went overboard pretending he was a dog. For a few days, he would only eat table scraps and insisted Momma put his water in a bowl so he could lap it.

The Best of Little Spouse on the Prairie

Almost every night before bedtime, Curry and I would beg Daddy to tickle us. Daddy learned the best way to get out of it was to make us cry right off, then Momma would make him stop. But we could get him to tell us war stories for hours on end. He'd tell us about the blackouts in London and digging foxholes in Belgium. But my favorite was when he would describe how they'd shut the engines off on the ship that carried him over to Europe when German subs were in the area. Daddy said he felt, any minute, a big torpedo was going to come through the wall and into his bunk!

I still remember all those stories by heart.

In the summertime, we'd put on our swim suits and Daddy would squirt us with the water hose. We'd run and squeal under the spray of water. We also liked to make "mud pies," but we were much too cultured to call them that. Instead, we called our mud creations "Indian pottery."

Like I said, my brother and I were awfully busy, making believe and making memories. Now, tell me that isn't more fun than a closet full of toys!

ORDER FORM

You have enjoyed reading about the adventures of: Mel, Ol' Green, Homer the bull and many more. Lana has not only given us a satirical look at modern day ranch life, but also a description of life with which we can all identify. No matter if you live on a ranch, a farm, in the big city or in suburbia, Lana offers something for **everyone**. Purchase copies of **THE BEST OF LITTLE SPOUSE ON THE PRAIRIE** for friends and relatives.

YES, please send _____ copies of **THE BEST OF LITTLE SPOUSE ON THE PRAIRIE** (@ $9.95 each) to the following:
(Enclosed is a check/money order for payment)

(Please Print)
NAME:_____

STREET ADDRESS/APT #:_____

P.O. BOX:_____

CITY:_____ STATE:_____ ZIP:_____

TELEPHONE NUMBER:_____
(In case we have a question about your order)

QTY	TITLE	UNIT PRICE	TOTAL AMOUNT
	THE BEST OF LITTLE SPOUSE ON THE PRAIRIE	$9.95	
	Postage & Handling ($2.00 per book)		
	Texas residents add 7.25% sales tax		
	*** TOTAL**		

* Send completed order form and make payment to:

BEDFORD HOUSE
P.O. Box 210726
Bedford, Texas 76095

(Allow 3-4 weeks for delivery)

ORDER FORM

You have enjoyed reading about the adventures of: Mel, Ol' Green, Homer the bull and many more. Lana has not only given us a satirical look at modern day ranch life, but also a description of life with which we can all identify. No matter if you live on a ranch, a farm, in the big city or in suburbia, Lana offers something for **everyone**. Purchase copies of **THE BEST OF LITTLE SPOUSE ON THE PRAIRIE** for friends and relatives.

YES, please send _____ copies of **THE BEST OF LITTLE SPOUSE ON THE PRAIRIE** (@ $9.95 each) to the following:
(Enclosed is a check/money order for payment)

(Please Print)
NAME:_____

STREET ADDRESS/APT #:_____

P.O. BOX:_____

CITY:_____ STATE:_____ ZIP:_____

TELEPHONE NUMBER:_____
(In case we have a question about your order)

QTY	TITLE	UNIT PRICE	TOTAL AMOUNT
	THE BEST OF LITTLE SPOUSE ON THE PRAIRIE	$9.95	
	Postage & Handling ($2.00 per book)		
	Texas residents add 7.25% sales tax		
	* TOTAL		

* Send completed order form and make payment to:

BEDFORD HOUSE
P.O. Box 210726
Bedford, Texas 76095

(Allow 3-4 weeks for delivery)

ORDER FORM

You have enjoyed reading about the adventures of: Mel, Ol' Green, Homer the bull and many more. Lana has not only given us a satirical look at modern day ranch life, but also a description of life with which we can all identify. No matter if you live on a ranch, a farm, in the big city or in suburbia, Lana offers something for **everyone**. Purchase copies of **THE BEST OF LITTLE SPOUSE ON THE PRAIRIE** for friends and relatives.

YES, please send _____ copies of **THE BEST OF LITTLE SPOUSE ON THE PRAIRIE** (@ $9.95 each) to the following:
(Enclosed is a check/money order for payment)

(Please Print)
NAME: _____

STREET ADDRESS/APT #: _____

P.O. BOX: _____

CITY: _____ STATE: _____ ZIP: _____

TELEPHONE NUMBER: _____
(In case we have a question about your order)

QTY	TITLE	UNIT PRICE	TOTAL AMOUNT
	THE BEST OF LITTLE SPOUSE ON THE PRAIRIE	$9.95	
	Postage & Handling ($2.00 per book)		
	Texas residents add 7.25% sales tax		
	*** TOTAL**		

* Send completed order form and make payment to:

BEDFORD HOUSE
P.O. Box 210726
Bedford, Texas 76095

(Allow 3-4 weeks for delivery)